BEETLE BAILEY:
KEEP PEELING

Here's another in the happy series of books based on one of the most famous comic strips in the country. Once again the madcap inmates of Camp Swampy valiantly strive to overcome their own ineptitude — and succeed in delighting us on every page.

Mort Walker again gives us a barrel of laughs in his marvelous cartoons concerning the most unprofessional soldier in the army!

Beetle Bailey Books

ABOUT FACE, BEETLE BAILEY
AT EASE, BEETLE BAILEY
BEETLE BAILEY: ANOTHER REQUEST FOR FURLOUGH
BEETLE BAILEY: BASKET CASE
BEETLE BAILEY: BEETLE BUGGED
BEETLE BAILEY: CORPORAL PUNISHMENT
BEETLE BAILEY: HARD KNOCKS
BEETLEY BAILEY: KEEP PEELING
BEETLE BAILEY: LET'S GRAB A BITE!
BEETLE BAILEY: NEW OUTFIT!
BEETLE BAILEY ON PARADE
BEETLE BAILEY: OPERATION GOOD TIMES
BEETLE BAILEY: TABLE SERVICE
BEETLE BAILEY: TATTLE "TAIL"
BEETLE BAILEY: WHA' HAPPEN?
BEETLE BAILEY: WIPED OUT
BEETLE BAILEY: WORLD'S LAZIEST PRIVATE
BIG HITS FROM BEETLE BAILEY
DID YOU FIX THE BRAKES, BEETLE BAILEY?
DON'T MAKE ME LAUGH, BEETLE BAILEY
FALL OUT LAUGHING, BEETLE BAILEY
GIVE US A SMILE, BEETLE BAILEY
I DON'T WANT TO BE OUT HERE
ANY MORE THAN YOU DO, BEETLE BAILEY
I'LL FLIP YOU FOR IT, BEETLE BAILEY
I JUST WANT TO TALK TO YOU, BEETLE BAILEY
IS THAT ALL, BEETLE BAILEY?
IS THIS ANOTHER COMPLAINT, BEETLE BAILEY?
I'VE GOT YOU ON MY LIST, BEETLE BAILEY
LET'S CHANGE PLACES, BEETLE BAILEY
LOOKIN' GOOD, BEETLE BAILEY
OTTO
PEACE, BEETLE BAILEY
SHAPE UP OR SHIP OUT, BEETLE BAILEY
TAKE A WALK, BEETLE BAILEY
TAKE TEN, BEETLE BAILEY
WE'RE ALL IN THE SAME BOAT, BEETLE BAILEY
WHAT IS IT NOW, BEETLE BAILEY?
WHAT'S THE JOKE, BEETLE BAILEY?
WHO'S IN CHARGE HERE, BEETLE BAILEY?
WOULD IT HELP TO SAY I'M SORRY, BEETLE BAILEY?
YOU'LL GET A BANG OUT OF THIS, BEETLE BAILEY
YOU'RE OUT OF HUP, BEETLE BAILEY?
YOU'RE ALL WASHED UP, BEETLE BAILEY

Keep Peeling

by Mort
WALKER

J
JOVE BOOKS, NEW YORK

BEETLE BAILEY: KEEP PEELING

A Jove Book / published by arrangement with
King Features Syndicate, Inc.

PRINTING HISTORY
Jove edition / March 1993

All rights reserved.
Copyright © 1990, 1993 by King Features Syndicate, Inc.
This book may not be reproduced in whole or in part,
by mimeograph or any other means, without permission.
For information address: The Berkley Publishing Group,
200 Madison Avenue, New York, New York 10016.

ISBN: 0-515-11086-8

Jove Books are published by The Berkley Publishing Group,
200 Madison Avenue, New York, New York 10016.
The name "JOVE" and the "J" logo
are trademarks belonging to Jove Publications, Inc.

PRINTED IN THE UNITED STATES OF AMERICA

10 9 8 7 6 5 4 3 2 1

BEETLE, WHY DO YOU SLEEP SO MUCH ?
I WAS A DEPRIVED CHILD
OH?... WHAT WERE YOU DEPRIVED OF?
SLEEP
MORT WALKER
1-29

WHAT IS HE DOING ?
OH, ZERO NEVER ADMITS HE DOESN'T KNOW HOW TO DO SOMETHING
1-30
SARGE TOLD HIM TO JUMP-START THE JEEP
MORT WALKER
© 1990 by King Features Syndicate Inc World rights reserved

THIS DRESS WILL NEVER GO OUT OF STYLE
REALLY?
1-31
IT HAS AN ADJUSTABLE HEMLINE
MORT WALKER

HE HAD A DATE IN TOWN BUT I **TOLD** HIM THE PLATOON WAS CONFINED TO THE BARRACKS
SEND HIM IN
2-1
WHAT'S THIS ABOUT YOU TRYING TO SNEAK OUT THROUGH THE HEATING PIPES, BEETLE?
MORT WALKER

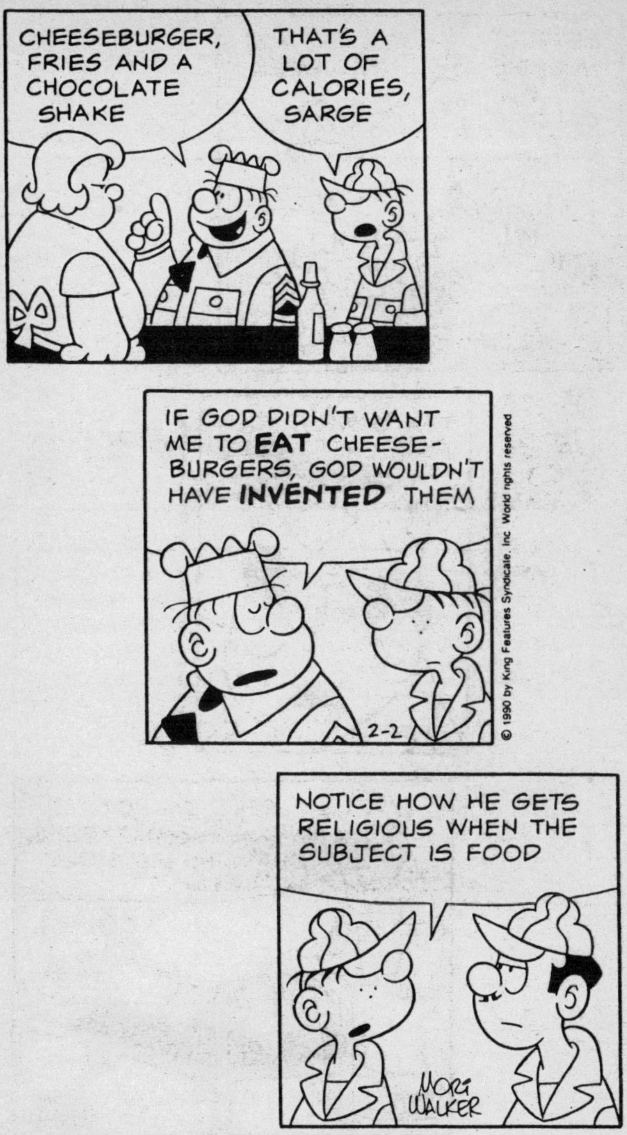
CHEESEBURGER, FRIES AND A CHOCOLATE SHAKE
THAT'S A LOT OF CALORIES, SARGE
IF GOD DIDN'T WANT ME TO EAT CHEESE-BURGERS, GOD WOULDN'T HAVE INVENTED THEM
2-2
© 1990 by King Features Syndicate, Inc World rights reserved
NOTICE HOW HE GETS RELIGIOUS WHEN THE SUBJECT IS FOOD
MORT WALKER

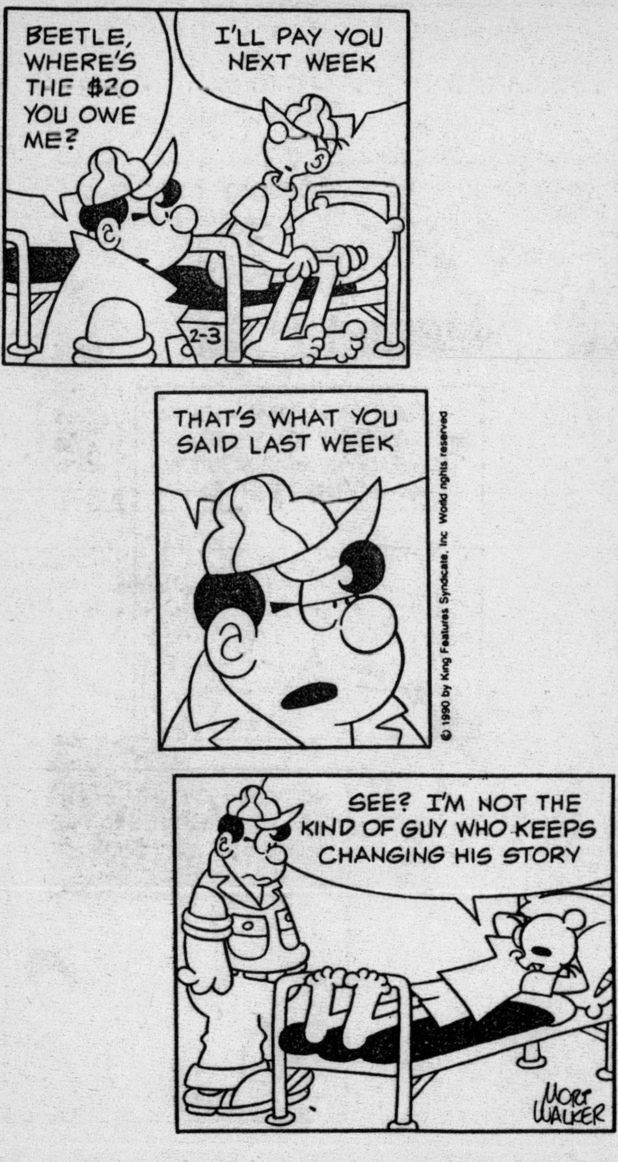
BEETLE, WHERE'S THE $20 YOU OWE ME?
I'LL PAY YOU NEXT WEEK
2-3
THAT'S WHAT YOU SAID LAST WEEK
SEE? I'M NOT THE KIND OF GUY WHO KEEPS CHANGING HIS STORY
MORT WALKER

WHAT'S THIS?
EVERYONE GETS ONE. IT'S CALLED "SARGE'S SWEEPSTAKES"
BEETLE
2-5
"YOU MAY ALREADY BE A WINNER!!! CHECK THE BULLETIN BOARD TO SEE IF YOU HAVE GARBAGE DUTY"
MORT WALKER

WHY DID YOU TELL ZERO TO KEEP ON HIS CAMOUFLAGE?
2-6
SOME BIRDS BUILT A NEST IN IT
MORT WALKER

2-7
WE USED OUR BEAUTIFICATION BUDGET ON TREES. WHAT DID YOU SPEND YOURS ON, AMOS?
NEW OFFICE PERSONNEL
MORT WALKER

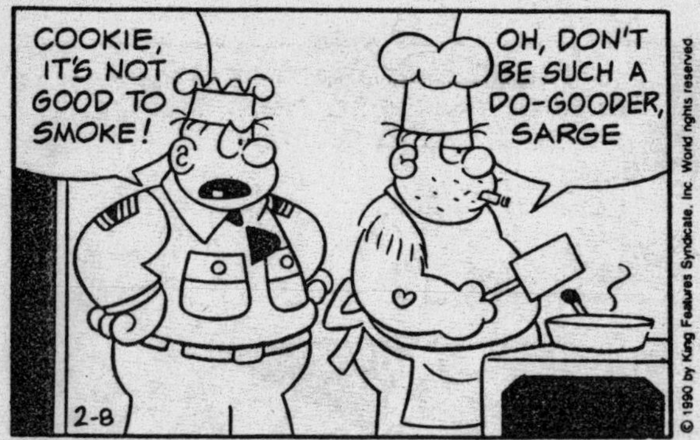
COOKIE, IT'S NOT GOOD TO SMOKE!
OH, DON'T BE SUCH A DO-GOODER, SARGE
2-8
© 1990 by King Features Syndicate, Inc. World rights reserved

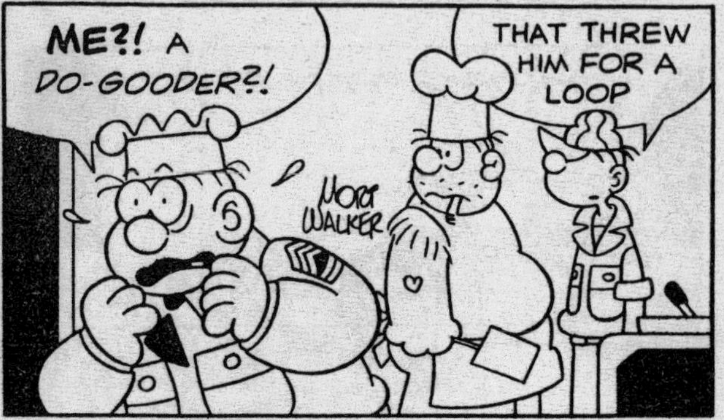
ME?! A DO-GOODER?!
THAT THREW HIM FOR A LOOP
MORT WALKER

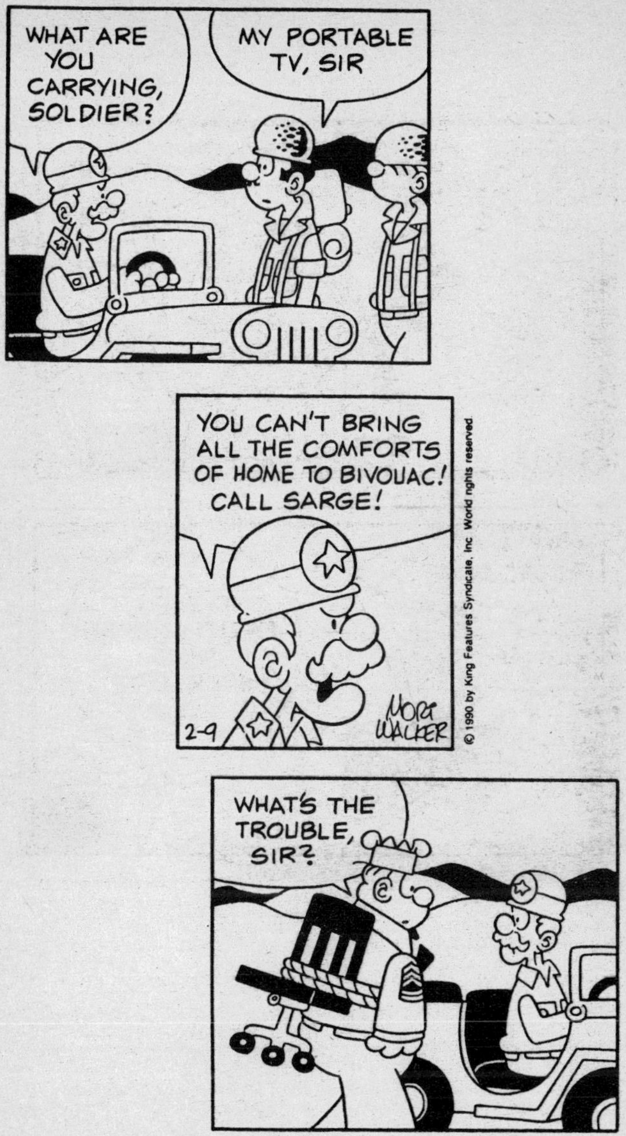
WHAT ARE YOU CARRYING, SOLDIER?
MY PORTABLE TV, SIR
YOU CAN'T BRING ALL THE COMFORTS OF HOME TO BIVOUAC! CALL SARGE!
2-9
MORT WALKER
WHAT'S THE TROUBLE, SIR?

ALL ACCOUNTED FOR EXCEPT BEETLE, SIR
IT FIGURES
2-10
HE EVEN **FALLS** SLOWER THAN EVERYONE ELSE
MORT WALKER

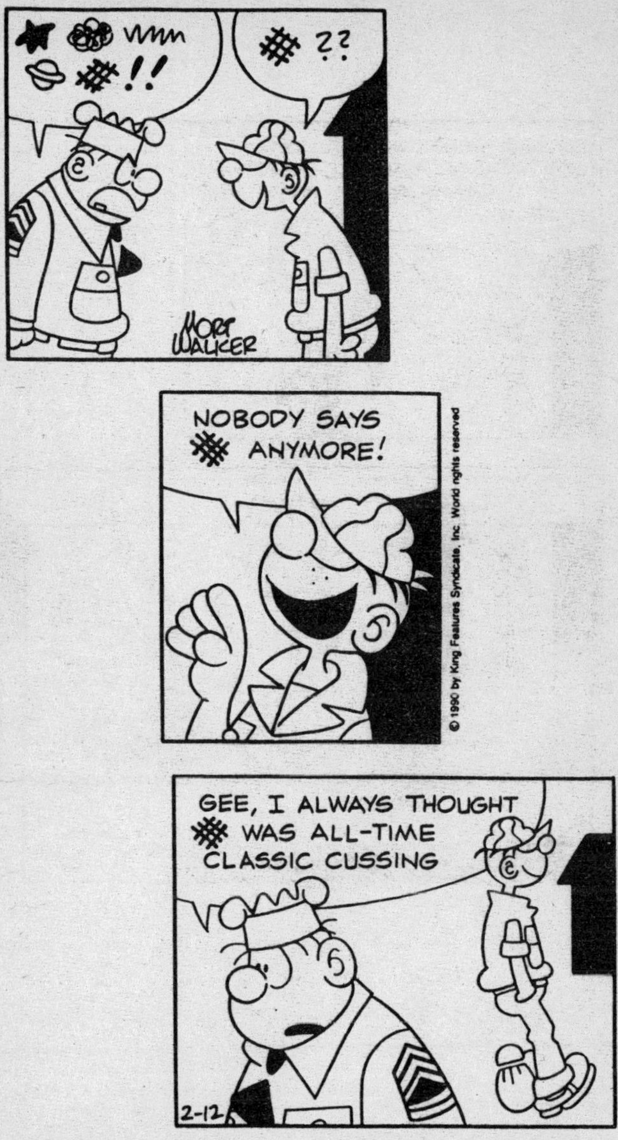
!!
??
MORT WALKER
NOBODY SAYS ANYMORE!
GEE, I ALWAYS THOUGHT WAS ALL-TIME CLASSIC CUSSING
2-12

LOUISE LUGG AND SGT. SNORKEL HAVE BEEN INSEPARABLE, LATELY
YES, I WONDER WHAT HER SECRET IS?
2-13
© 1990 by King Features Syndicate, Inc. World rights reserved
EPOXY
MORT WALKER

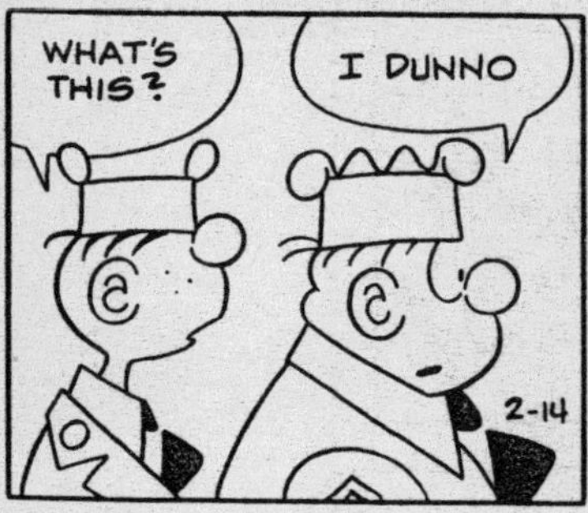
WHAT'S THIS?
I DUNNO
2-14

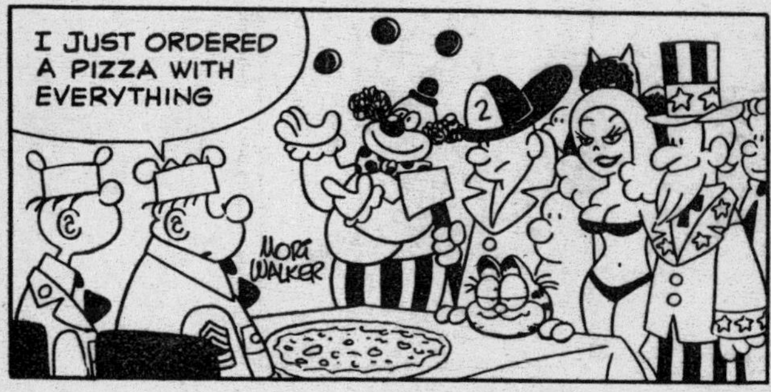
I JUST ORDERED A PIZZA WITH EVERYTHING
MORT WALKER

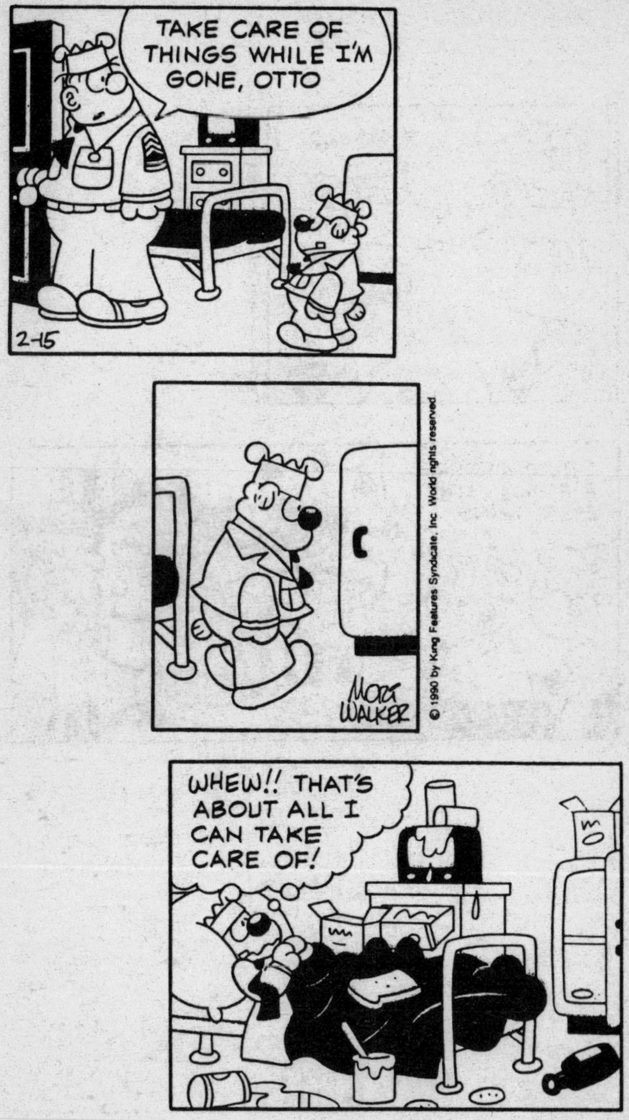
TAKE CARE OF THINGS WHILE I'M GONE, OTTO
2-15
MORT WALKER
WHEW!! THAT'S ABOUT ALL I CAN TAKE CARE OF!

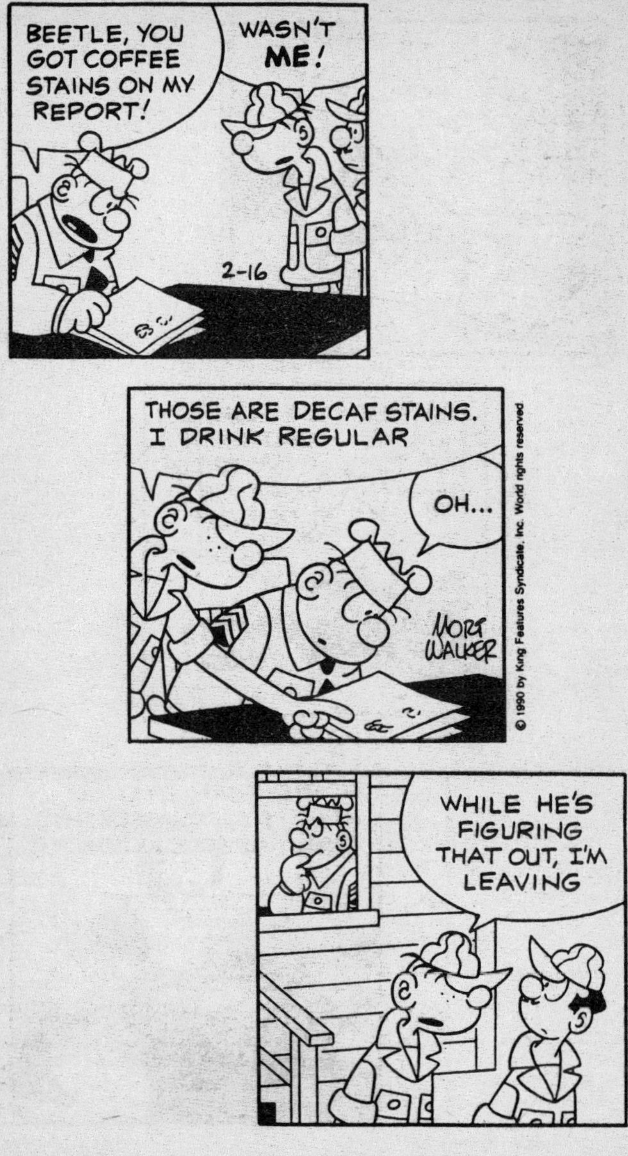
BEETLE, YOU GOT COFFEE STAINS ON MY REPORT!
WASN'T **ME**!
2-16
THOSE ARE DECAF STAINS. I DRINK REGULAR
OH...
MORT WALKER
WHILE HE'S FIGURING THAT OUT, I'M LEAVING

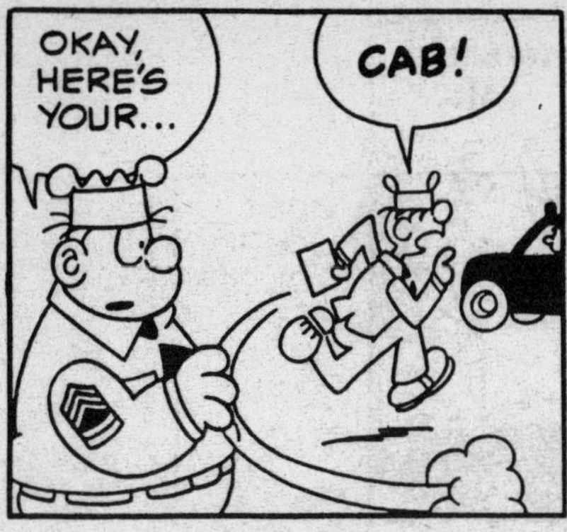
OKAY, HERE'S YOUR...
CAB!

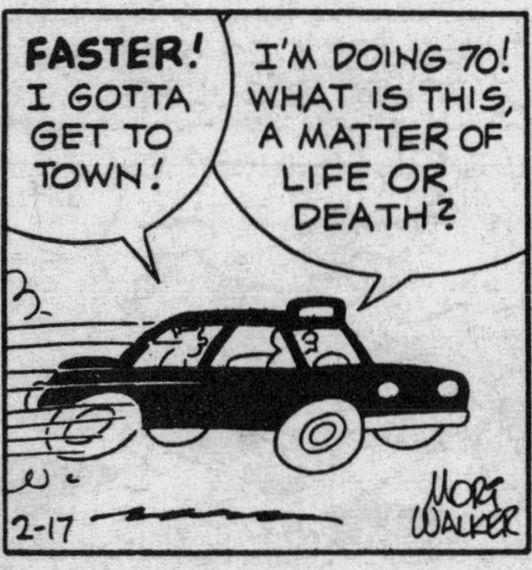
FASTER! I GOTTA GET TO TOWN!
I'M DOING 70! WHAT IS THIS, A MATTER OF LIFE OR DEATH?
2-17
MORT WALKER

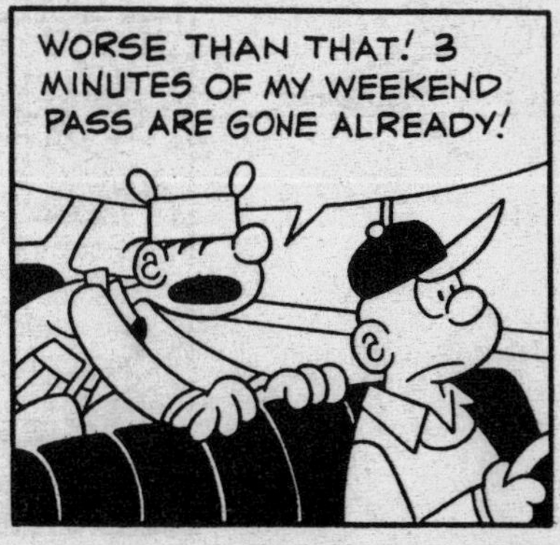
WORSE THAN THAT! 3 MINUTES OF MY WEEKEND PASS ARE GONE ALREADY!

COOKIE'S RAVING MAD BECAUSE WE COMPLAINED ABOUT HIS DINNER!
HE'S UP ON HIS ROOF!
I'M BUSY! JUST GO TRY TO COOL HIM OFF
2-19
© 1990 by King Features Syndicate, Inc. World rights reserved
OKAY, TURN IT ON
MORT WALKER

IT'S A NICE SIGN, ZERO, BUT I HAVE A SUGGESTION
2-20
SAW ALONG THAT DOTTED LINE
MORT WALKER
ONE WAY

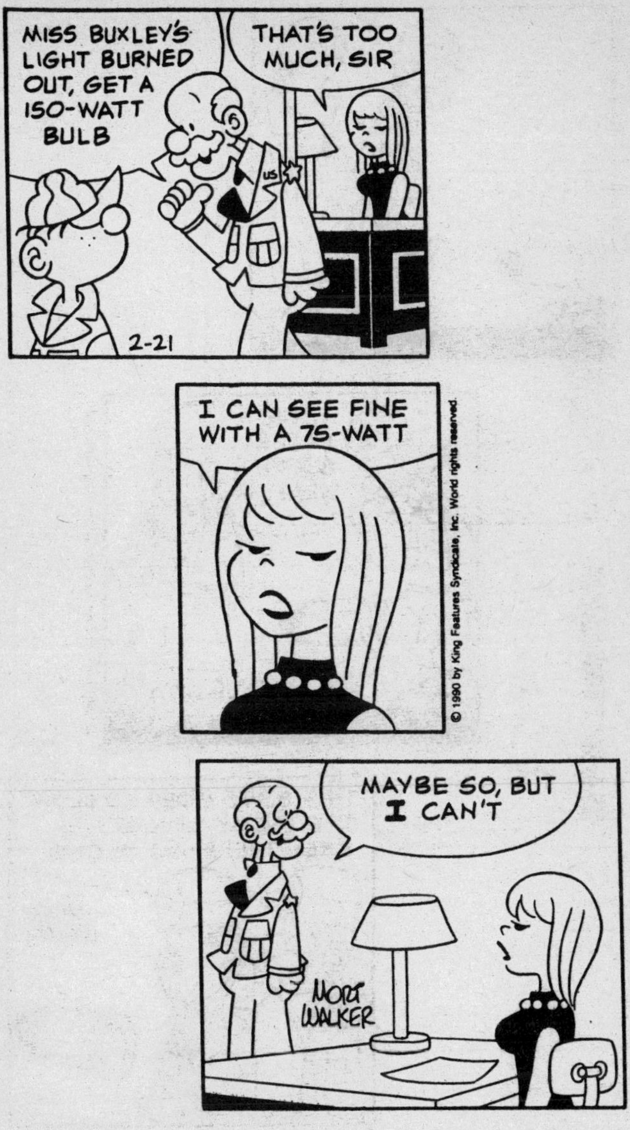
MISS BUXLEY'S LIGHT BURNED OUT, GET A 150-WATT BULB
THAT'S TOO MUCH, SIR
2-21
I CAN SEE FINE WITH A 75-WATT
MAYBE SO, BUT I CAN'T
MORT WALKER

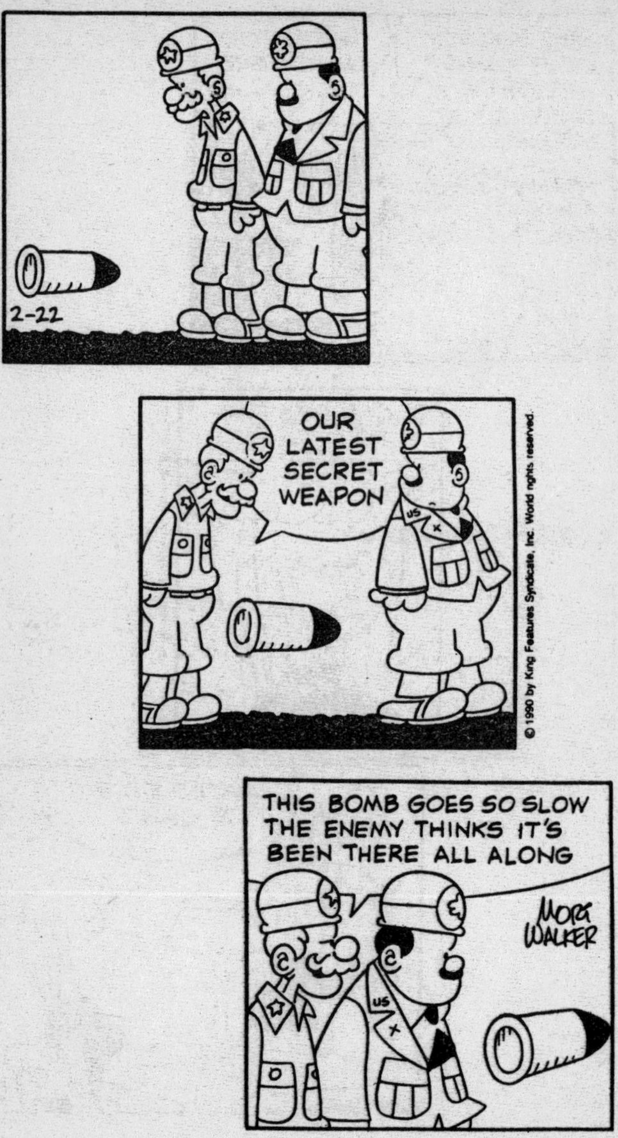
2-22
OUR LATEST SECRET WEAPON
THIS BOMB GOES SO SLOW THE ENEMY THINKS IT'S BEEN THERE ALL ALONG
MORT WALKER

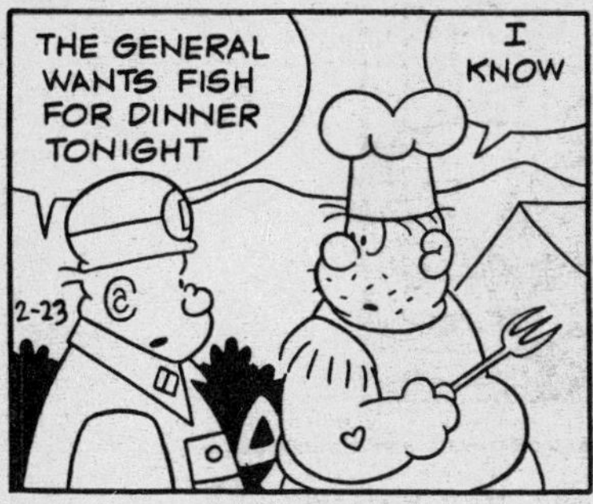
THE GENERAL WANTS FISH FOR DINNER TONIGHT
I KNOW
2-23

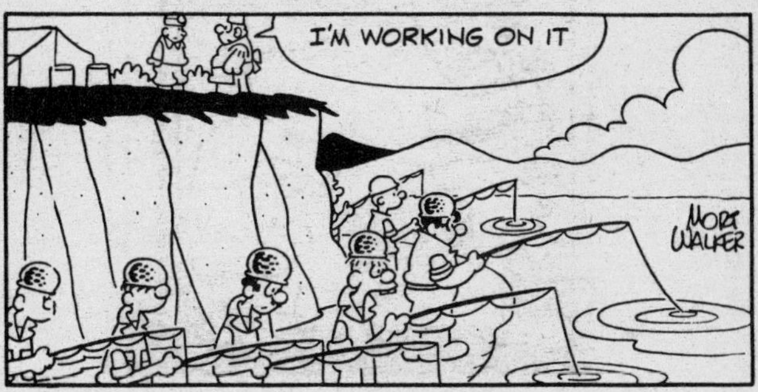
I'M WORKING ON IT
MORT WALKER

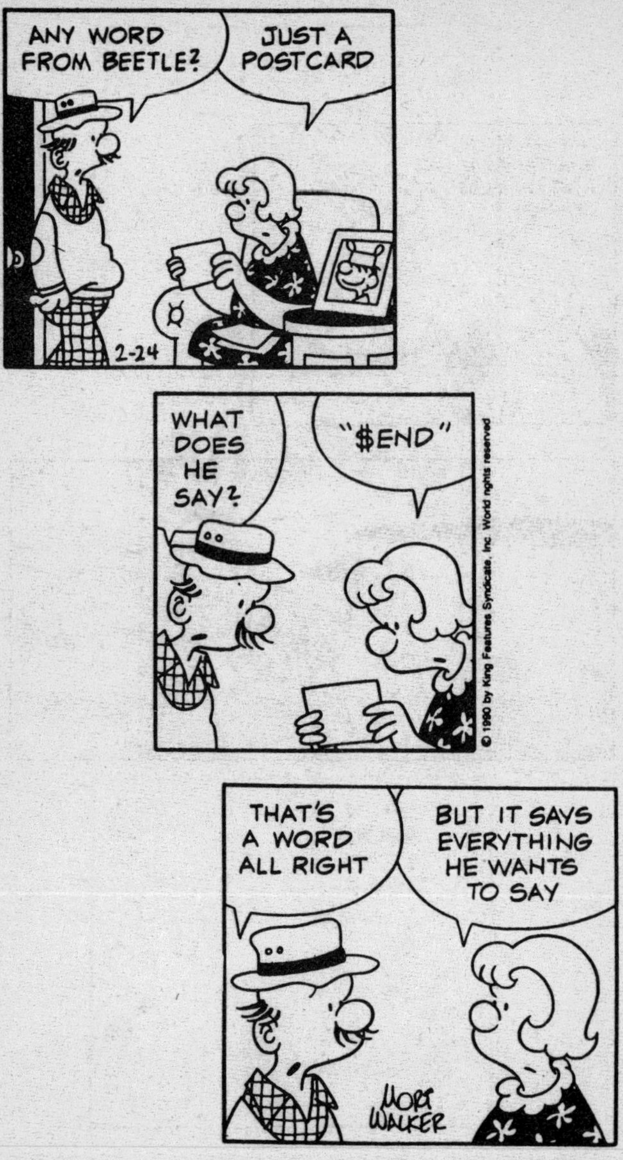
ANY WORD FROM BEETLE?
JUST A POSTCARD
2-24
WHAT DOES HE SAY?
"$END"
© 1990 by King Features Syndicate, Inc. World rights reserved
THAT'S A WORD ALL RIGHT
BUT IT SAYS EVERYTHING HE WANTS TO SAY
MORT WALKER

BEETLE, YOU MUST LEARN TO LOOK AT YOUR TROUBLES SQUARE IN THE FACE AND LAUGH AT THEM
2-26
HA HA HA HA
MORT WALKER
TALK ABOUT LOUSY ADVICE

WHY WON'T SARGE GIVE ME A TUMBLE?
MAYBE YOU'RE TOO EASY. TRY PLAYING HARD TO GET FOR A CHANGE
2-27
© 1990 by King Features Syndicate, Inc World rights reserved
YOO-HOO, SARGE! BET YOU CAN'T GET ME!
MORT WALKER

THERE GOES KILLER ON THE PROWL AGAIN
DOESN'T HE EVER GIVE UP?
2-28
Grille
I'D REALLY LIKE TO KNOW YOU BETTER
HERE, OR TO TAKE OUT?
MORT WALKER

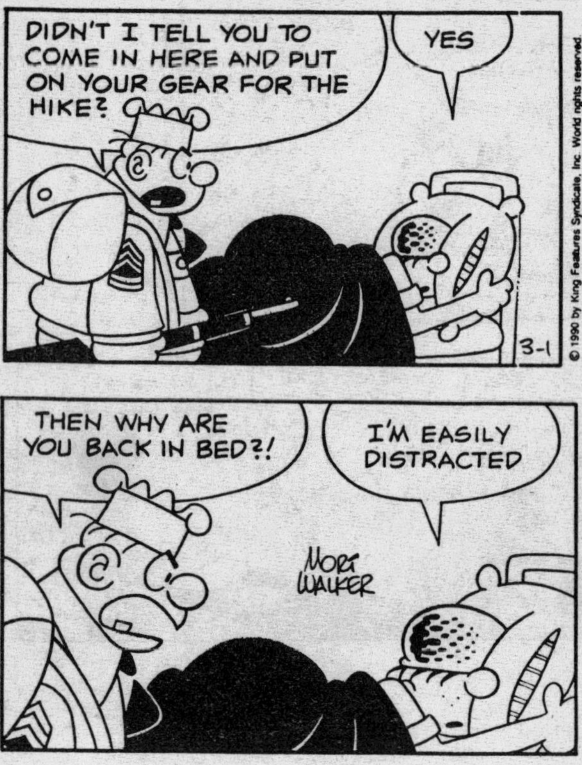
DIDN'T I TELL YOU TO COME IN HERE AND PUT ON YOUR GEAR FOR THE HIKE?
YES
3-1
THEN WHY ARE YOU BACK IN BED?!
I'M EASILY DISTRACTED
MORT WALKER

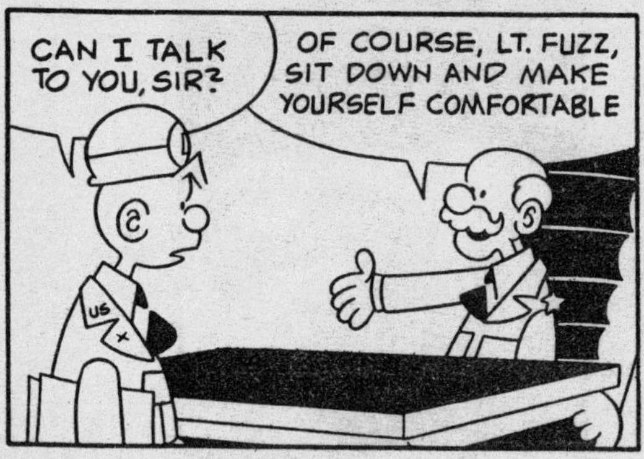
CAN I TALK TO YOU, SIR?
OF COURSE, LT. FUZZ, SIT DOWN AND MAKE YOURSELF COMFORTABLE

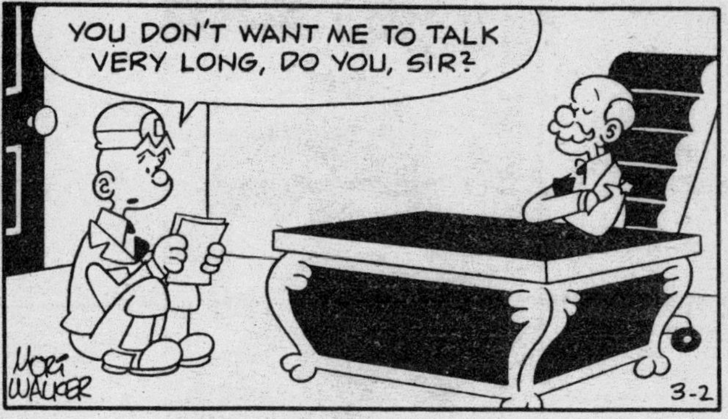
YOU DON'T WANT ME TO TALK VERY LONG, DO YOU, SIR?
MORT WALKER
3-2

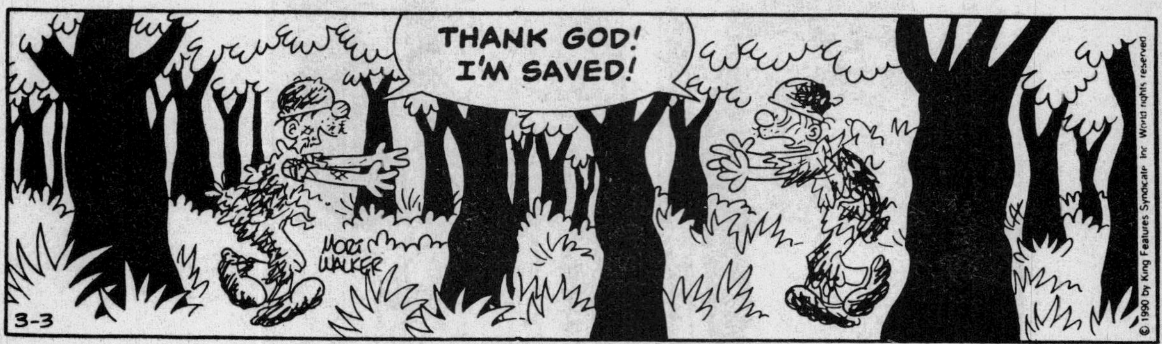
THANK GOD! I'M SAVED!
MORT WALKER
3-3
© 1990 by King Features Syndicate Inc. World rights reserved

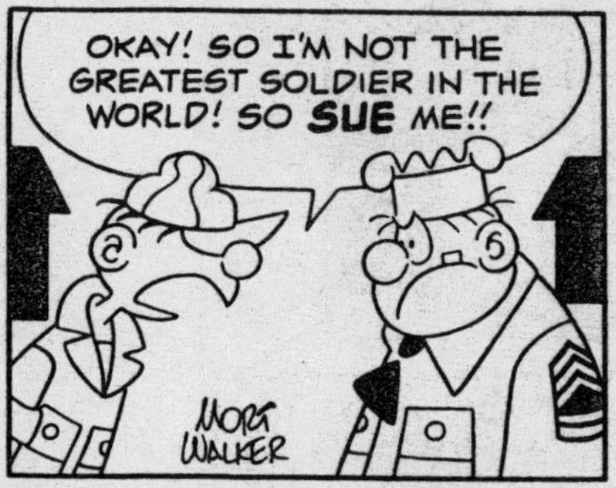
OKAY! SO I'M NOT THE GREATEST SOLDIER IN THE WORLD! SO **SUE** ME!!
MORT WALKER

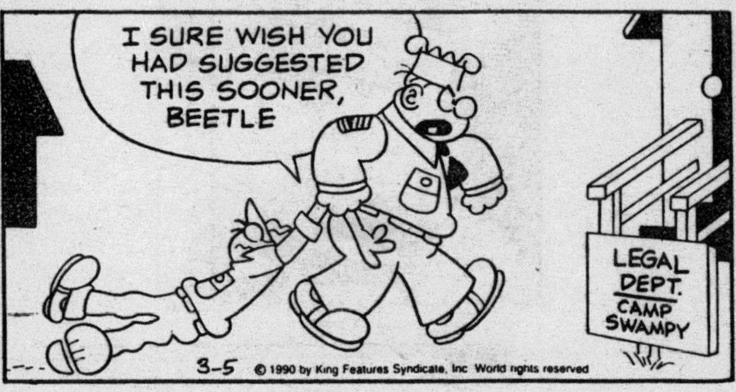
I SURE WISH YOU HAD SUGGESTED THIS SOONER, BEETLE
LEGAL DEPT.
CAMP SWAMPY
3-5
© 1990 by King Features Syndicate, Inc World rights reserved

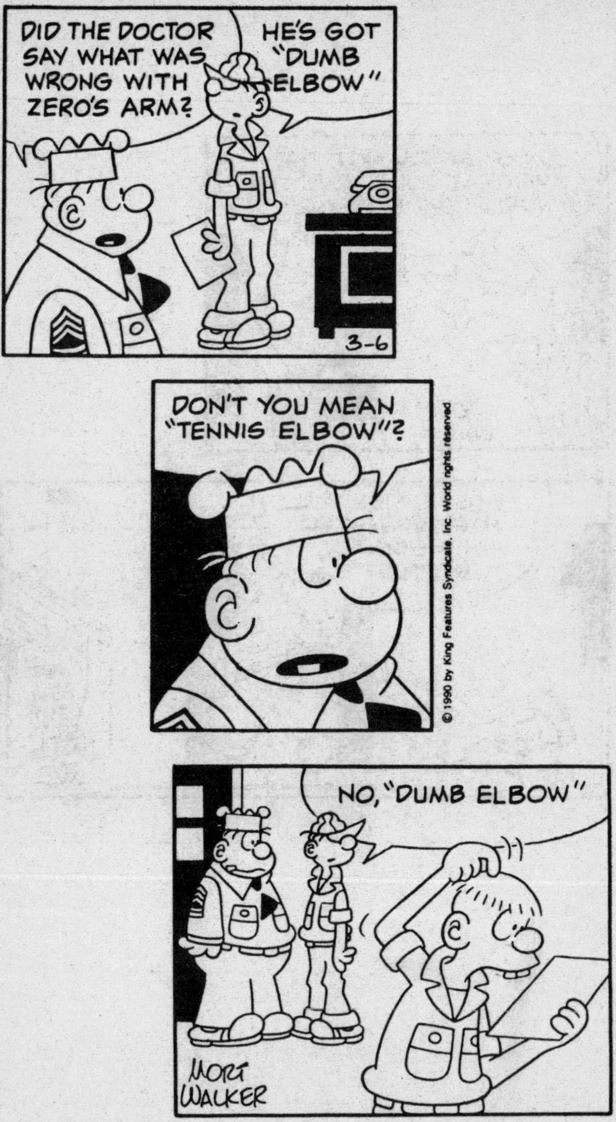
DID THE DOCTOR SAY WHAT WAS WRONG WITH ZERO'S ARM?
HE'S GOT "DUMB ELBOW"
3-6
DON'T YOU MEAN "TENNIS ELBOW"?
NO, "DUMB ELBOW"
MORT WALKER

JUST A MINUTE, SIR, I'LL GET THE FUZZ OFF YOUR JACKET
3-7
THANKS. NOW IF I COULD JUST GET LT. FUZZ OUT OF MY **HAIR**
US
MORT WALKER
© 1990 by King Features Syndicate, Inc. World rights reserved

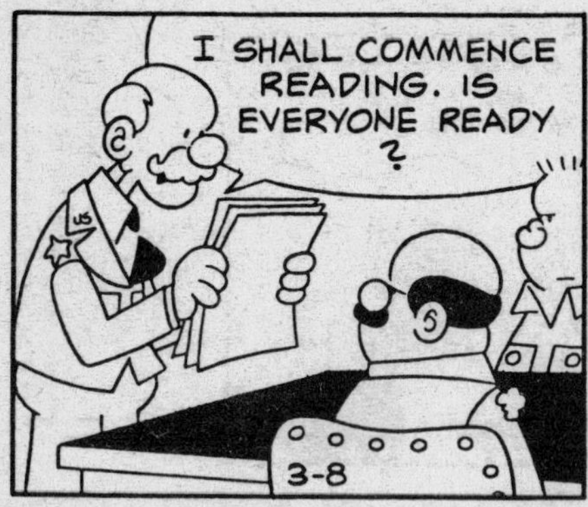
I SHALL COMMENCE READING. IS EVERYONE READY?
3-8

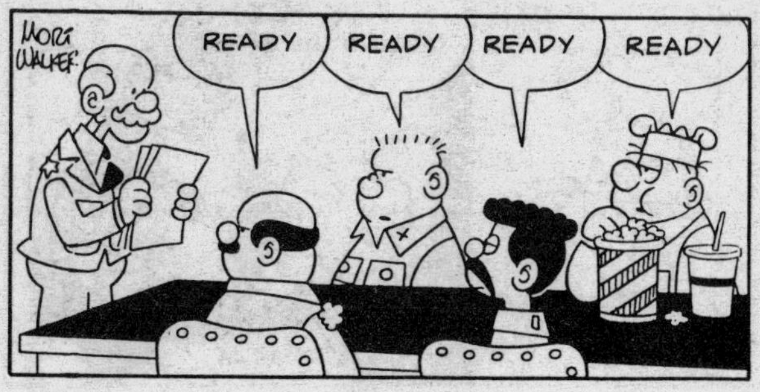
MORT WALKER
READY
READY
READY
READY

I'M TIRED, DIRTY AND HUNGRY. CAN I MAKE A SANDWICH?
OKAY
3-9
HOLD IT. DID YOU WASH YOUR HANDS?
WHAT DO **YOU** THINK?
MORT WALKER

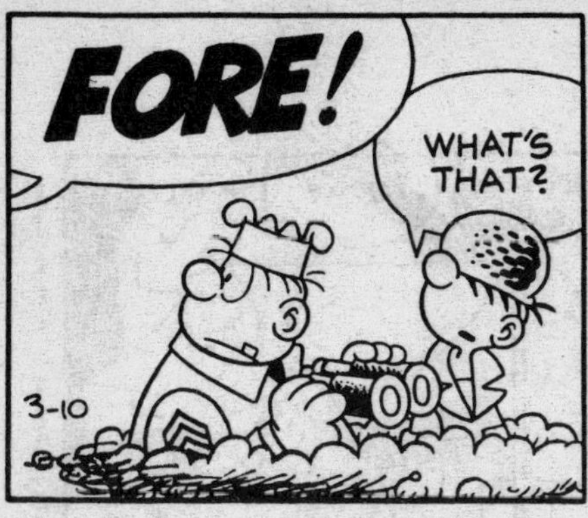
FORE!
WHAT'S THAT?
3-10

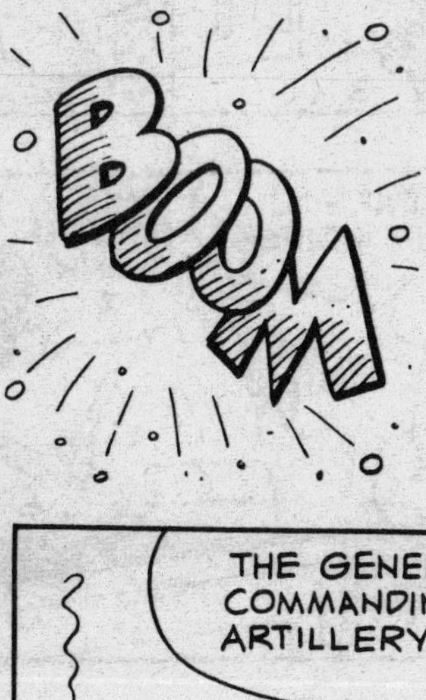
BOOM

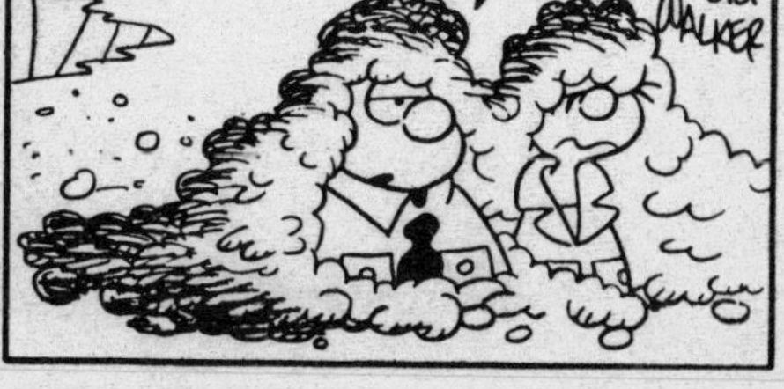
THE GENERAL IS COMMANDING THE ARTILLERY TODAY
MORT WALKER

I NEED TWO VOLUNTEERS. THE GENERAL WANTS TO MAKE NOTES ON THE BOMBARDMENT
CAN'T HE WRITE BY HIMSELF?
3-14
BOOM
BAM
MORT WALKER
© 1990 by King Features Syndicate, Inc. World rights reserved

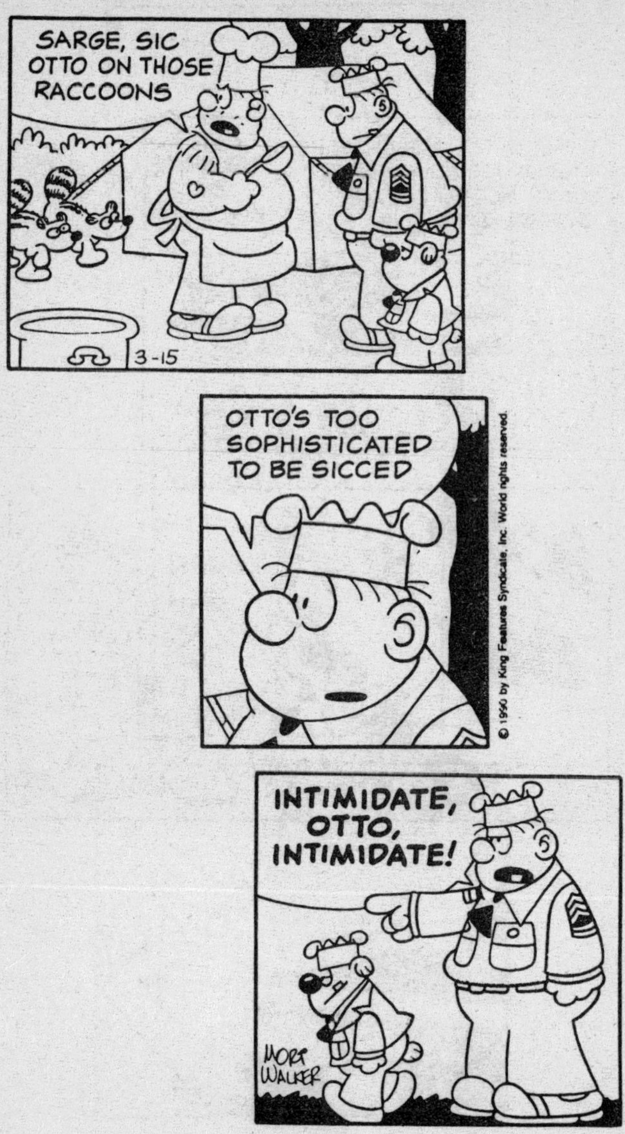
SARGE, SIC OTTO ON THOSE RACCOONS
3-15
OTTO'S TOO SOPHISTICATED TO BE SICCED
INTIMIDATE, OTTO, INTIMIDATE!
MORT WALKER

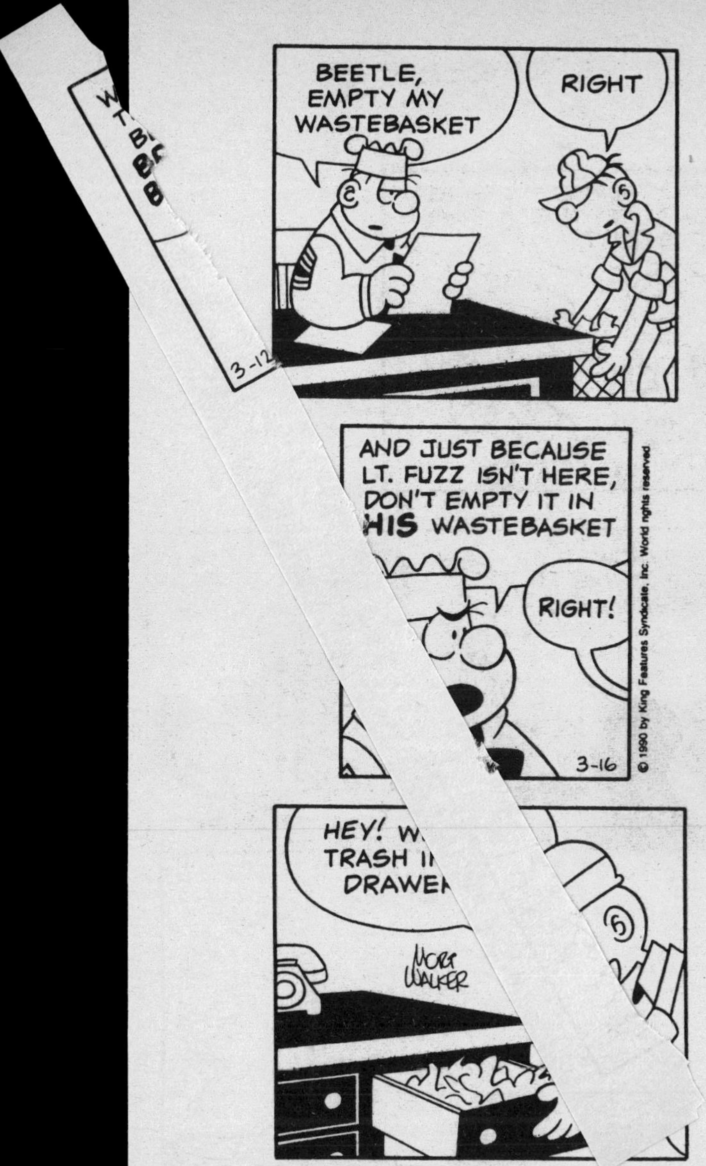
BEETLE, EMPTY MY WASTEBASKET
RIGHT
3-12
AND JUST BECAUSE LT. FUZZ ISN'T HERE, DON'T EMPTY IT IN HIS WASTEBASKET
RIGHT!
3-16
HEY!
TRASH
MORT WALKER

OH-OH! THEY'RE GOING TO TRY THE "BEETLE BLITZ"!
WHAT'S THAT?
3-17
THEY THROW BEETLE AT THE QUARTERBACK
MORT WALKER
© 1990 by King Features Syndicate, Inc. World rights reserved

I DON'T KNOW WHAT'S WRONG WITH YOU GUYS!
FIRST YOU DAWDLE OVER YOUR COLD CUTS
NOW YOU'RE NOT EATING YOUR ICE CREAM!
3-19
MORT WALKER

Y'KNOW WHAT I HATE MOST ABOUT WINTER?
WHAT?
US
A BUNDLED-UP MISS BUXLEY
MORT WALKER
3-20

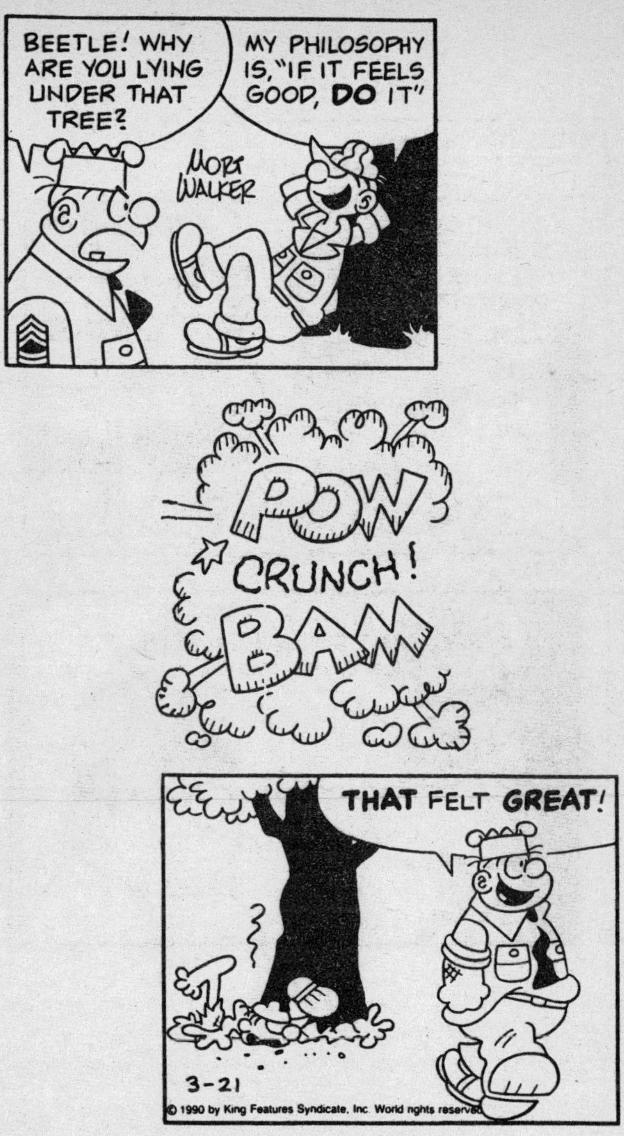
BEETLE! WHY ARE YOU LYING UNDER THAT TREE?
MY PHILOSOPHY IS, "IF IT FEELS GOOD, DO IT"
MORT WALKER
POW
CRUNCH!
BAM
THAT FELT GREAT!
3-21
© 1990 by King Features Syndicate, Inc. World rights reserv

KILLER GOT A SPEEDING TICKET WHILE HE WAS PARKED
A **SPEEDING** TICKET WHILE HE WAS **PARKED** ?!
3-22
YEAH, HE WAS MOVING TOO FAST ON HIS DATE IN A DRIVE-IN MOVIE
MORT WALKER
© 1990 by King Features Syndicate Inc World rights reserved

BAM BAM BAM BAM BAM BAM BAM BAM
THE MEN ARE GIVING YOU A 21-GUN SALUTE, SIR
I'VE COUNTED 30 SO FAR
BAM! BAM! BAM!
ZERO ALWAYS GETS CARRIED AWAY
MORT WALKER
3-23

HEY, SARGE, YOU TOLD **US** NOT TO PUT PENS OR PENCILS IN OUR SHIRT POCKETS
THESE AREN'T PENS OR PENCILS
3-24
THEY'RE FRENCH FRIES
MORT WALKER

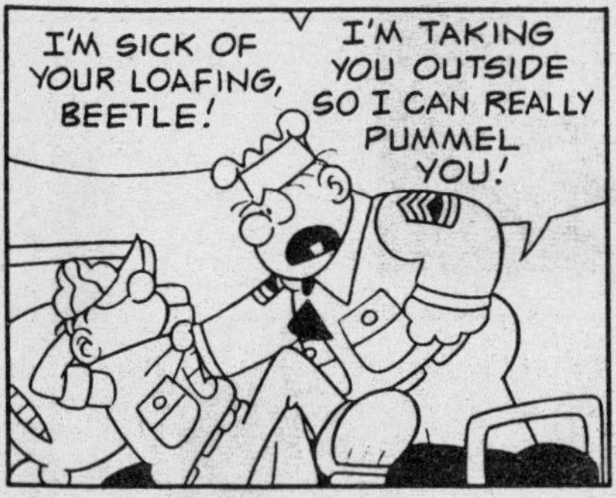
I'M SICK OF YOUR LOAFING, BEETLE!
I'M TAKING YOU OUTSIDE SO I CAN REALLY PUMMEL YOU!

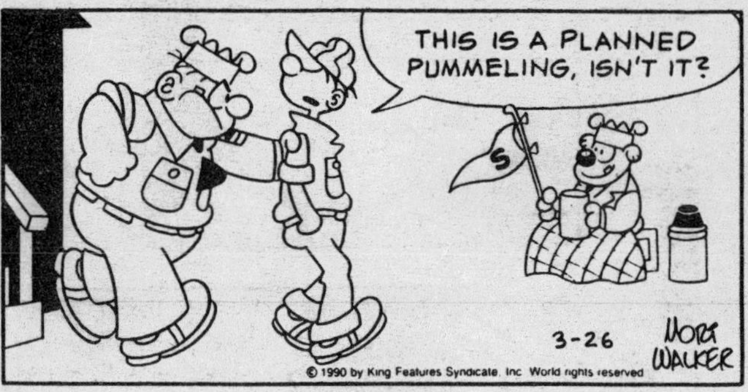
THIS IS A PLANNED PUMMELING, ISN'T IT?
3-26
MORT WALKER
© 1990 by King Features Syndicate, Inc. World rights reserved

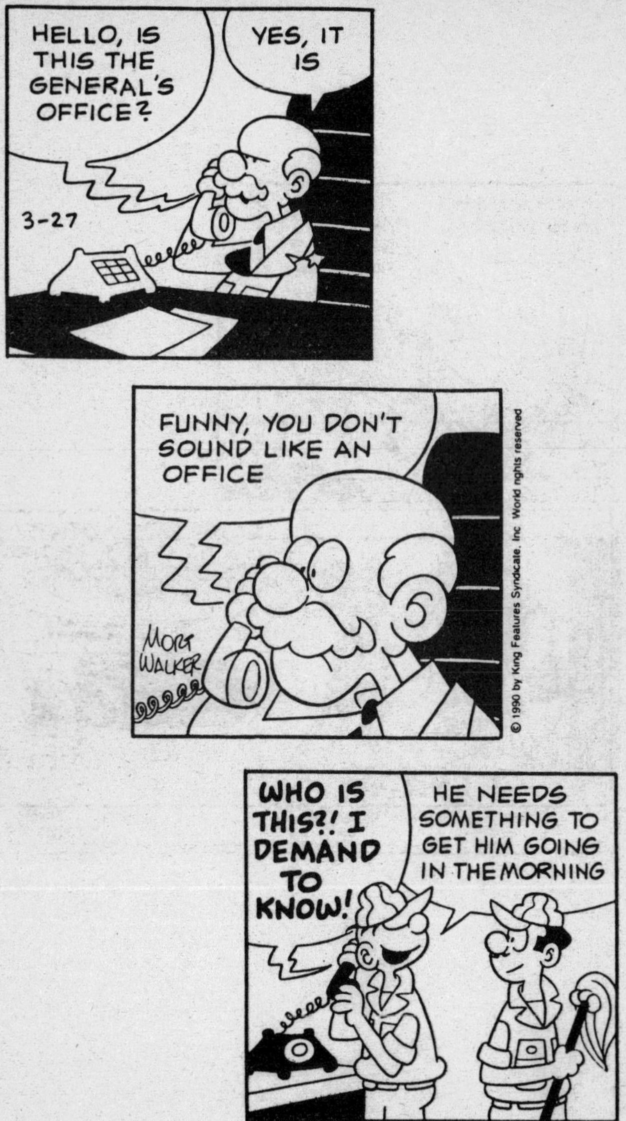
HELLO, IS THIS THE GENERAL'S OFFICE?
YES, IT IS
3-27
FUNNY, YOU DON'T SOUND LIKE AN OFFICE
MORT WALKER
WHO IS THIS?! I DEMAND TO KNOW!
HE NEEDS SOMETHING TO GET HIM GOING IN THE MORNING

TAKE A MEMO, MISS BUXLEY...
TO THE PERSONNEL OF CAMP SWAMPY...
3-28
LATELY, I'VE NOTICED THAT NO ONE IS TAKING HIS JOB SERIOUSLY ENOUGH
MORT WALKER
© 1990 by King Features Syndicate, Inc. World rights reserved

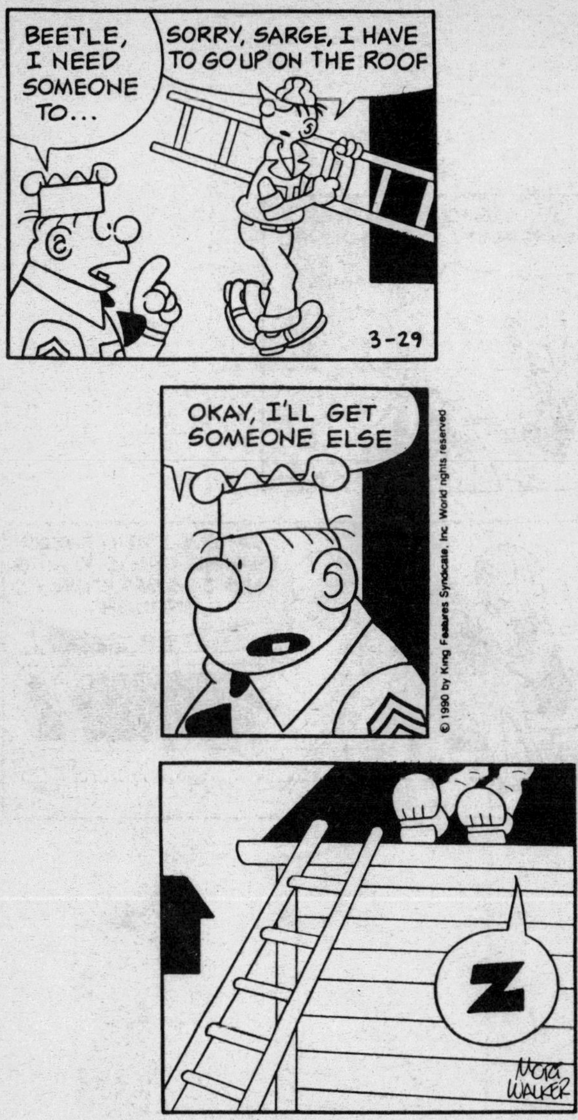
BEETLE, I NEED SOMEONE TO...
SORRY, SARGE, I HAVE TO GO UP ON THE ROOF
3-29
OKAY, I'LL GET SOMEONE ELSE
Z
MORT WALKER

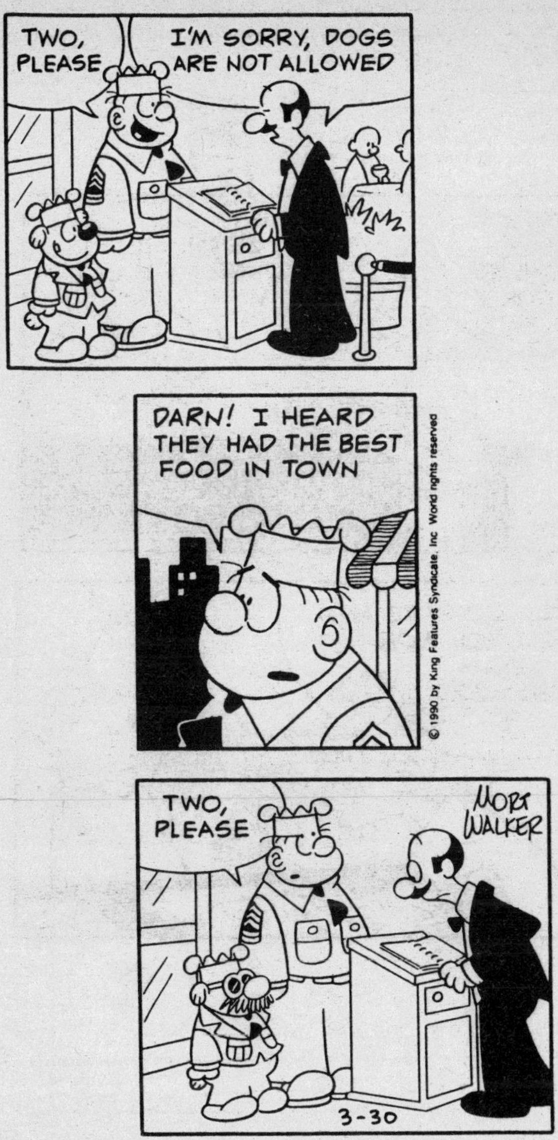

TWO, PLEASE
I'M SORRY, DOGS ARE NOT ALLOWED
DARN! I HEARD THEY HAD THE BEST FOOD IN TOWN
TWO, PLEASE
MORT WALKER
3-30

WHAT'S FOR DINNER, COOKIE ?
A REAL TREAT, ZERO... SMOKED SALMON!
3-31
© 1990 by King Features Syndicate, Inc. World rights reserved.
DO YOU HAVE ANY SALMON FOR NON-SMOKERS ?
MORT WALKER

GET UP, BEETLE!!
MORT WALKER
(SIGH) ANOTHER DAY, ANOTHER HOLLER
4-2
© 1990 by King Features Syndicate, Inc. World rights reserved

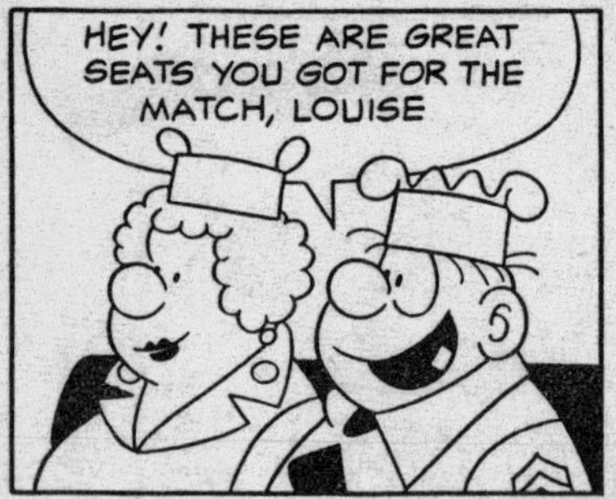
HEY! THESE ARE GREAT SEATS YOU GOT FOR THE MATCH, LOUISE

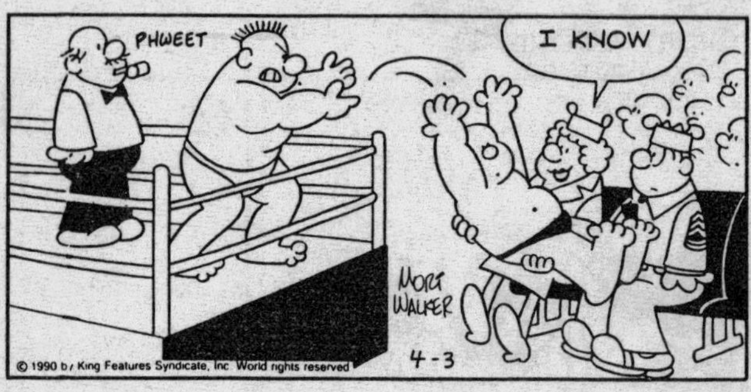
PHWEET
I KNOW
MORT WALKER
4-3
© 1990 by King Features Syndicate, Inc. World rights reserved

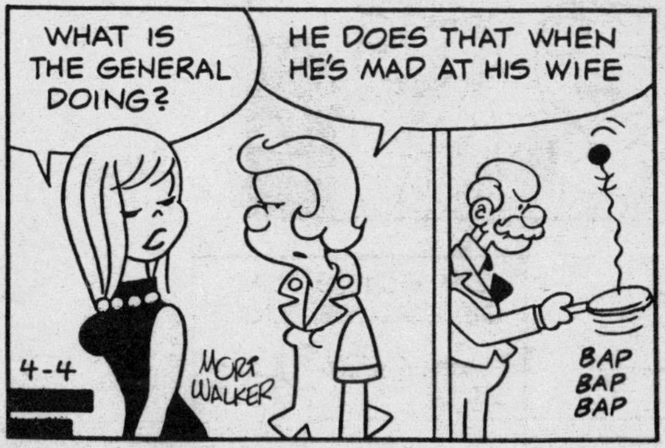
WHAT IS THE GENERAL DOING?
HE DOES THAT WHEN HE'S MAD AT HIS WIFE
4-4
MORT WALKER
BAP BAP BAP

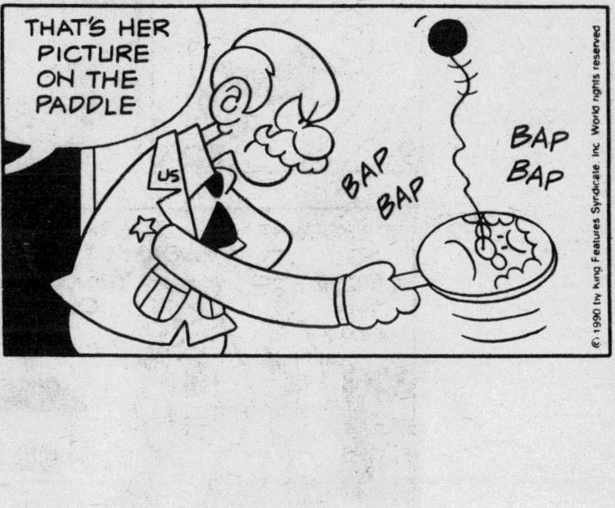
THAT'S HER PICTURE ON THE PADDLE
US
BAP BAP
BAP BAP

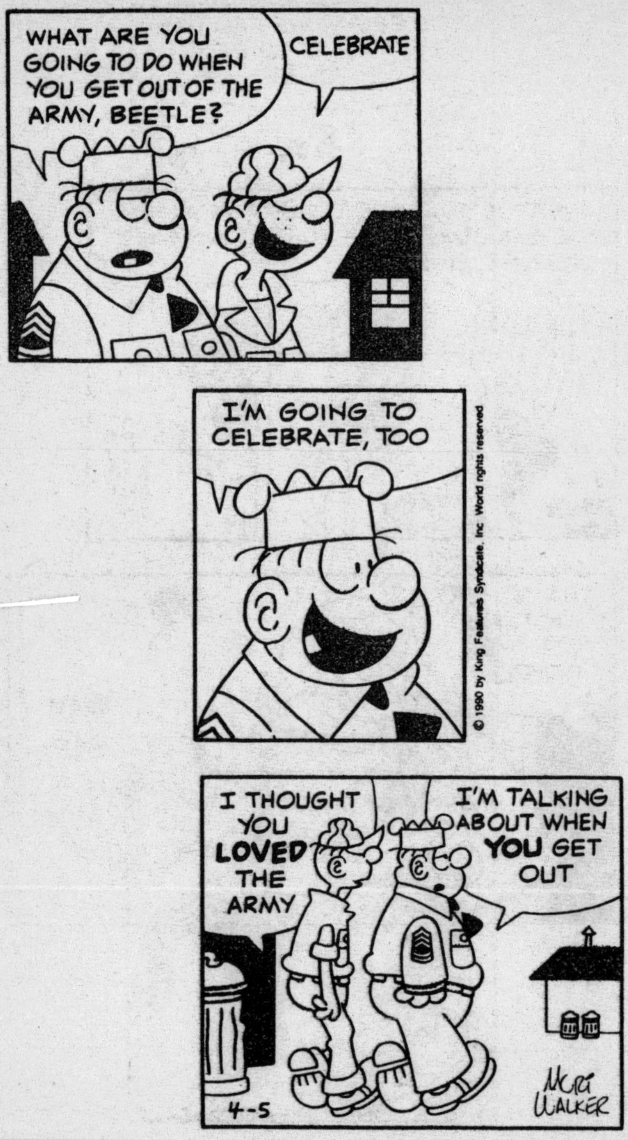
WHAT ARE YOU GOING TO DO WHEN YOU GET OUT OF THE ARMY, BEETLE?
CELEBRATE
I'M GOING TO CELEBRATE, TOO
I THOUGHT YOU **LOVED** THE ARMY
I'M TALKING ABOUT WHEN **YOU** GET OUT
4-5
MORT WALKER

LET'S SEE IF WE CAN USE HER PHONE TO GET BEETLE TO JOIN US
4-6
THIS PHONE CAN ONLY BE USED FOR BUSINESS
RIGHT
MORT WALKER
I'M TRYING TO FORM A MERGER WITH A MAJOR HOLDOUT TO ABSORB LIQUID ASSETS
OH, GO AHEAD

WHAT'S THIS?
IT'S A COMBINATION OF WHOLESOME, PREVIOUSLY PREPARED FOODSTUFFS.
MORT WALKER
HE CAN'T MAKE HIMSELF SAY "LEFTOVERS."
4-7

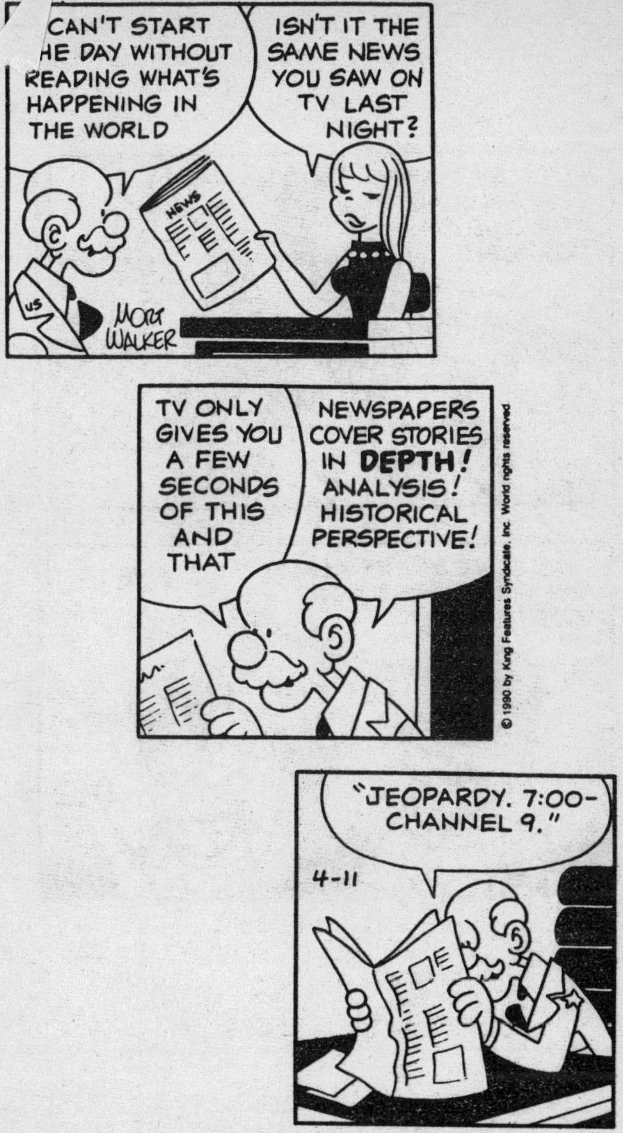
CAN'T START HE DAY WITHOUT READING WHAT'S HAPPENING IN THE WORLD
ISN'T IT THE SAME NEWS YOU SAW ON TV LAST NIGHT?
NEWS
US
MORT WALKER
TV ONLY GIVES YOU A FEW SECONDS OF THIS AND THAT
NEWSPAPERS COVER STORIES IN **DEPTH**! ANALYSIS! HISTORICAL PERSPECTIVE!
"JEOPARDY. 7:00- CHANNEL 9."
4-11

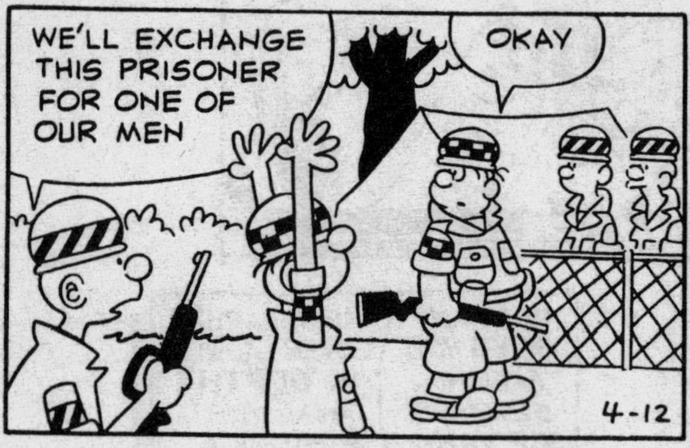
WE'LL EXCHANGE THIS PRISONER FOR ONE OF OUR MEN
OKAY
4-12

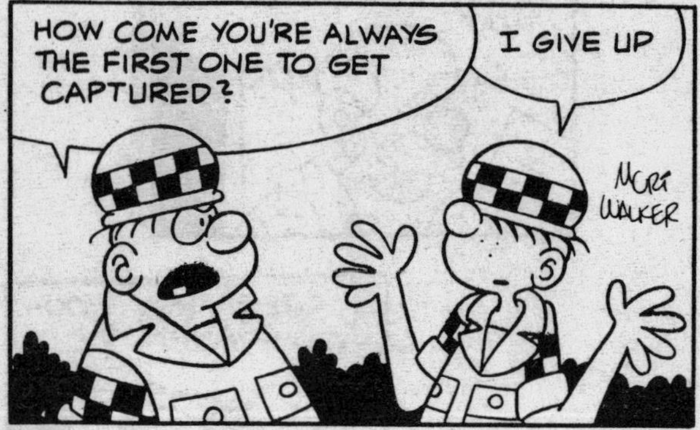
HOW COME YOU'RE ALWAYS THE FIRST ONE TO GET CAPTURED?
I GIVE UP
MORT WALKER

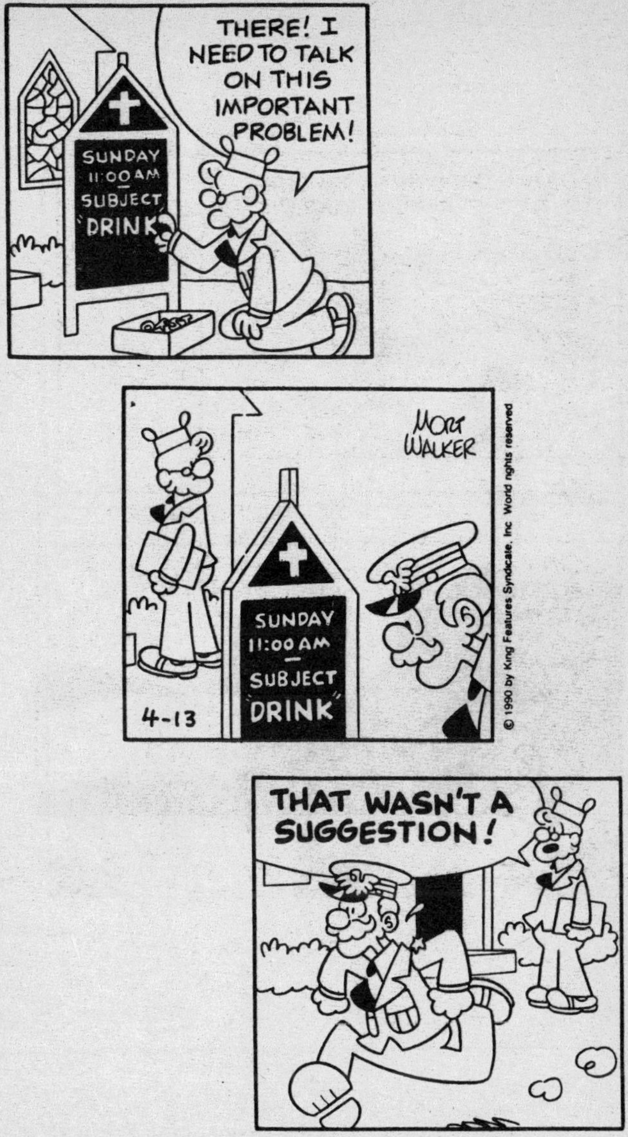
THERE! I NEED TO TALK ON THIS IMPORTANT PROBLEM!
SUNDAY
11:00 AM
SUBJECT
DRINK
MORT WALKER
SUNDAY
11:00 AM
SUBJECT
"DRINK"
4-13
THAT WASN'T A SUGGESTION!

IT'S BAD ENOUGH THAT THE GENERAL ORDERED A BIVOUAC THE DAY OF THE BIG GAME...
4-14
BUT THEN HE TAKES THE SPOT WITH THE BEST RECEPTION
MORT WALKER
© 1990 by King Features Syndicate, Inc.

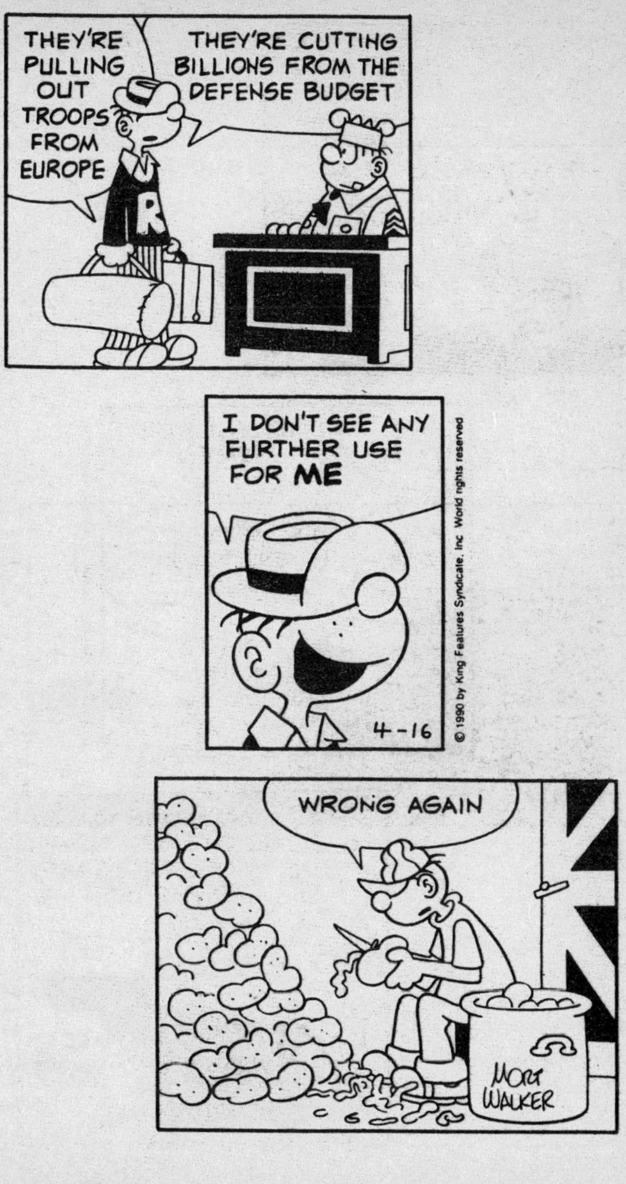
THEY'RE PULLING OUT TROOPS FROM EUROPE
THEY'RE CUTTING BILLIONS FROM THE DEFENSE BUDGET
I DON'T SEE ANY FURTHER USE FOR ME
4-16
WRONG AGAIN
MORT WALKER

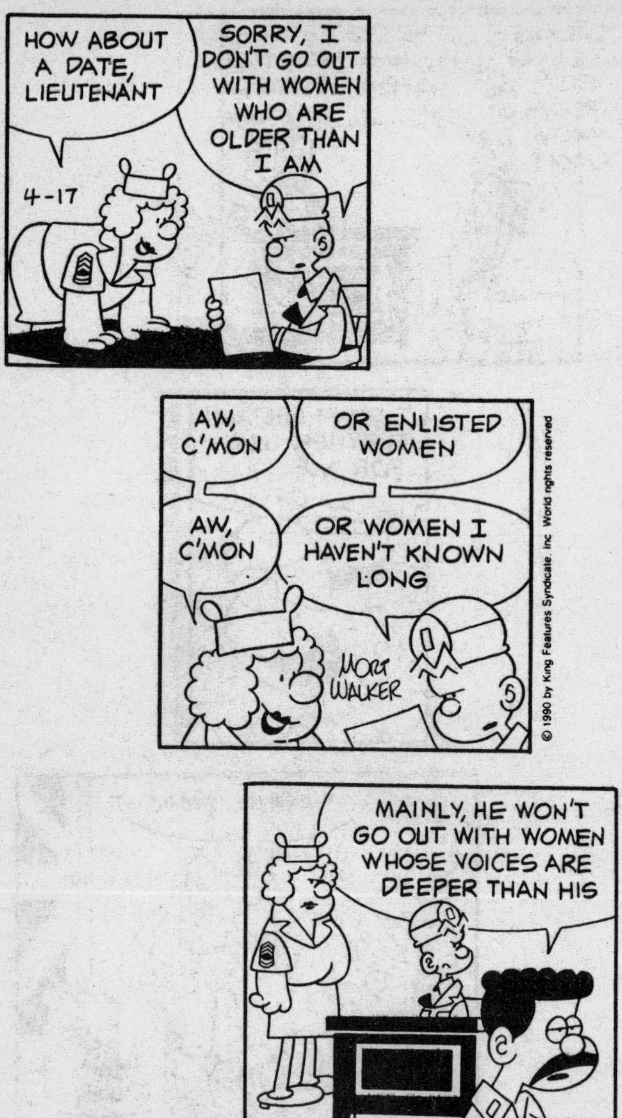
HOW ABOUT A DATE, LIEUTENANT
SORRY, I DON'T GO OUT WITH WOMEN WHO ARE OLDER THAN I AM
4-17
AW, C'MON
OR ENLISTED WOMEN
AW, C'MON
OR WOMEN I HAVEN'T KNOWN LONG
MORT WALKER
MAINLY, HE WON'T GO OUT WITH WOMEN WHOSE VOICES ARE DEEPER THAN HIS

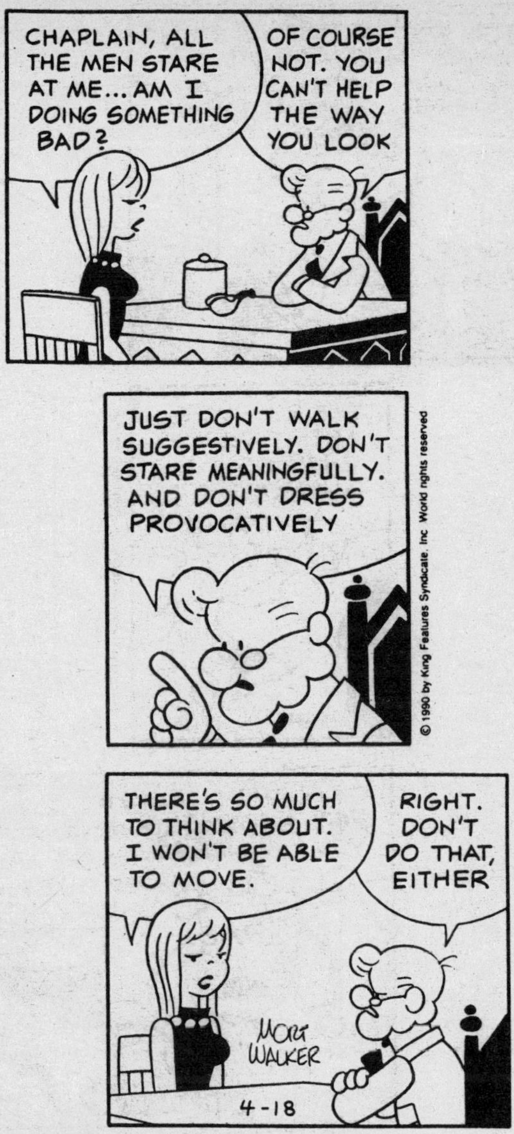
CHAPLAIN, ALL THE MEN STARE AT ME... AM I DOING SOMETHING BAD?
OF COURSE NOT. YOU CAN'T HELP THE WAY YOU LOOK
JUST DON'T WALK SUGGESTIVELY. DON'T STARE MEANINGFULLY. AND DON'T DRESS PROVOCATIVELY
THERE'S SO MUCH TO THINK ABOUT. I WON'T BE ABLE TO MOVE.
RIGHT. DON'T DO THAT, EITHER
MORT WALKER
4-18

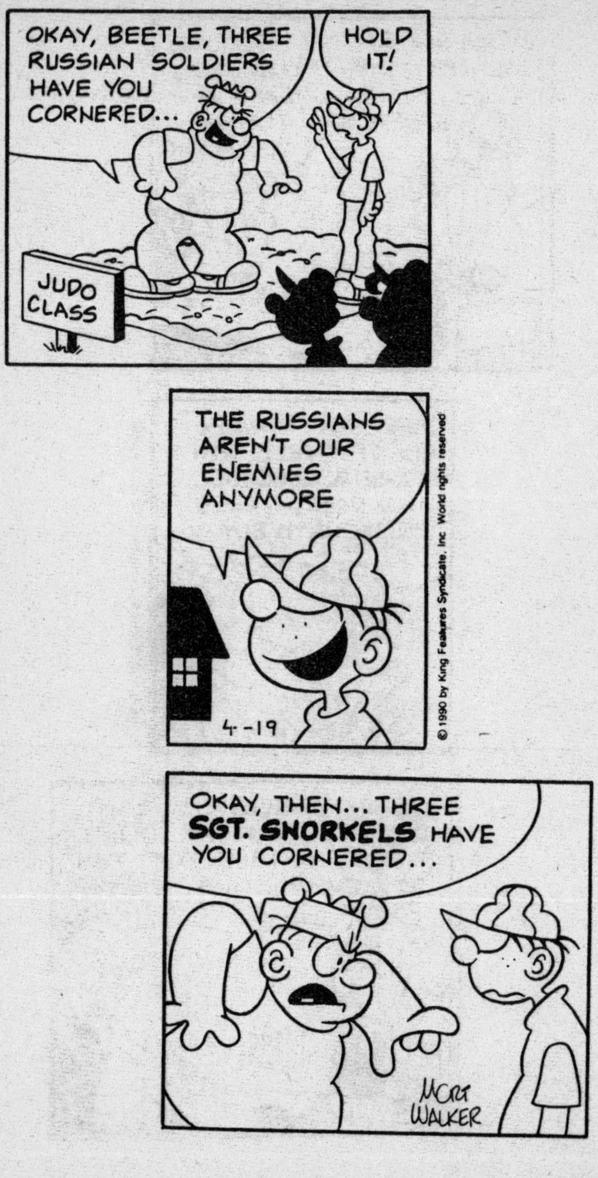

OKAY, BEETLE, THREE RUSSIAN SOLDIERS HAVE YOU CORNERED...
HOLD IT!
JUDO CLASS
THE RUSSIANS AREN'T OUR ENEMIES ANYMORE
4-19
OKAY, THEN... THREE **SGT. SNORKELS** HAVE YOU CORNERED...
MORT WALKER

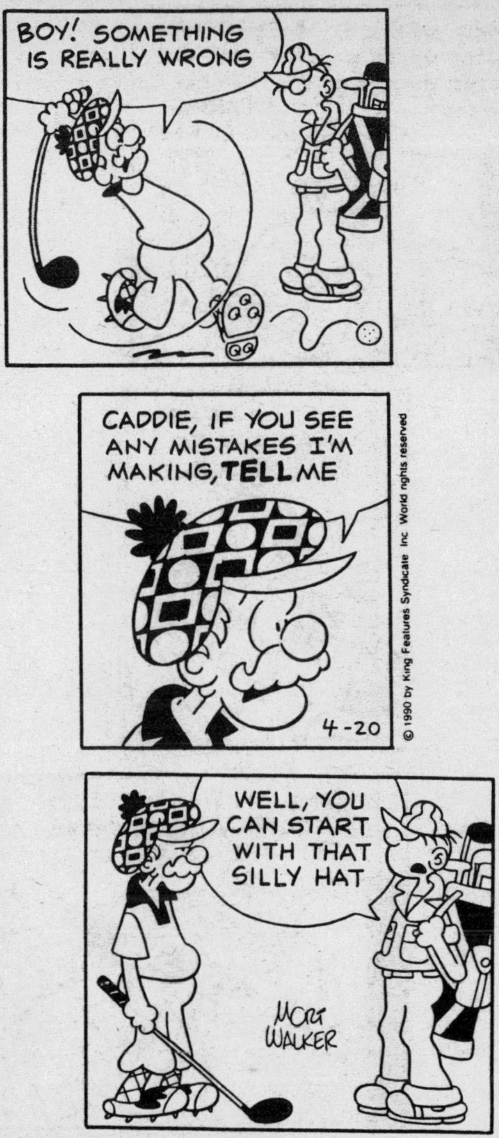
BOY! SOMETHING IS REALLY WRONG
CADDIE, IF YOU SEE ANY MISTAKES I'M MAKING, TELL ME
4-20
WELL, YOU CAN START WITH THAT SILLY HAT
MORT WALKER

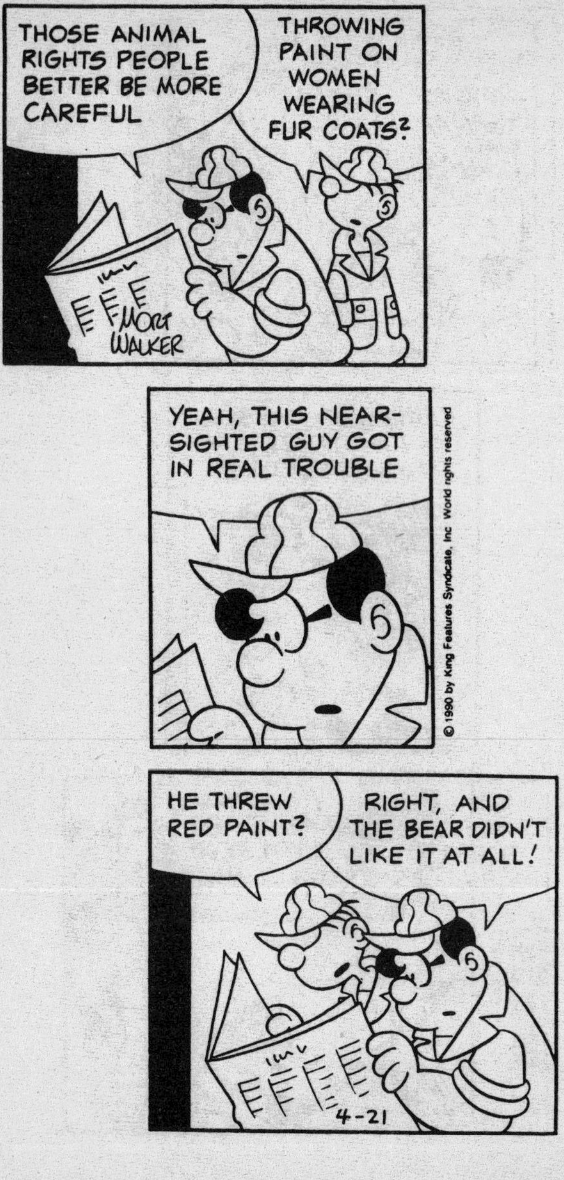
THOSE ANIMAL RIGHTS PEOPLE BETTER BE MORE CAREFUL
THROWING PAINT ON WOMEN WEARING FUR COATS?
MORT WALKER
YEAH, THIS NEAR-SIGHTED GUY GOT IN REAL TROUBLE
HE THREW RED PAINT?
RIGHT, AND THE BEAR DIDN'T LIKE IT AT ALL!
4-21

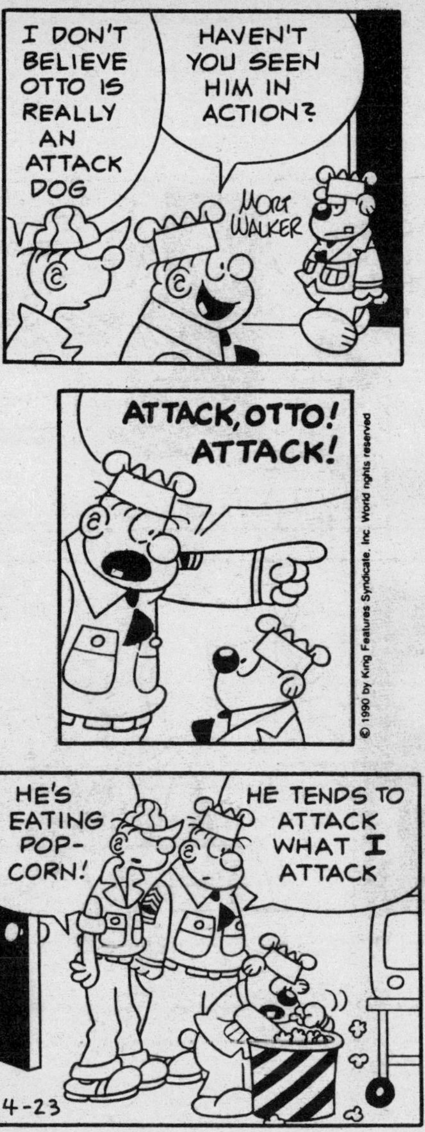
I DON'T BELIEVE OTTO IS REALLY AN ATTACK DOG
HAVEN'T YOU SEEN HIM IN ACTION?
MORT WALKER
ATTACK, OTTO! ATTACK!
HE'S EATING POP-CORN!
HE TENDS TO ATTACK WHAT I ATTACK
4-23

SARGE AND LUGG LOVE THIS DEAL, "ALL YOU CAN EAT FOR $10."
TELL THE CHEF TO KEEP IT COMING
4-24
© 1990 by King Features Syndicate, Inc. World rights reserved
MORT WALKER

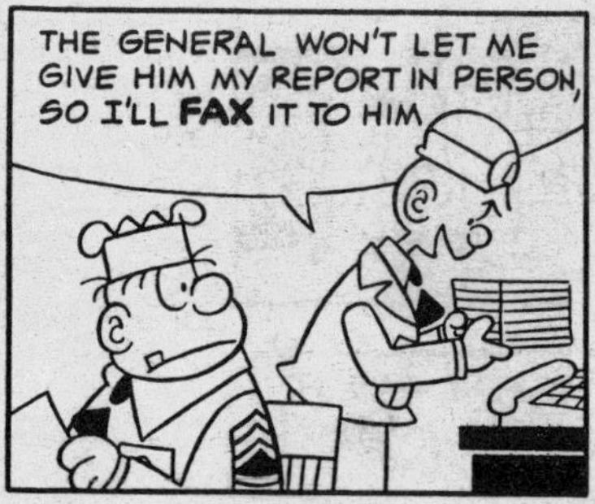
THE GENERAL WON'T LET ME GIVE HIM MY REPORT IN PERSON, SO I'LL FAX IT TO HIM

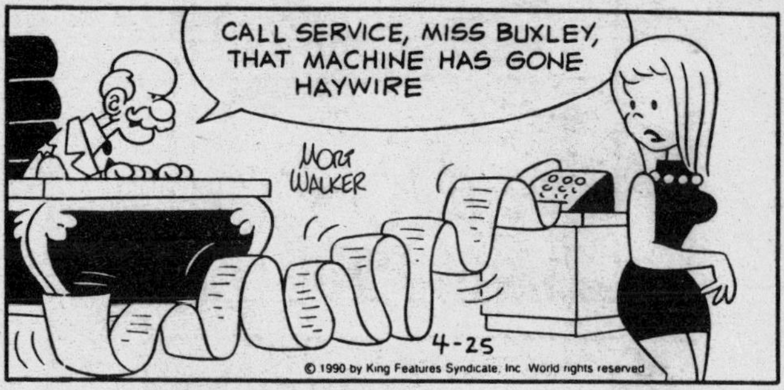
CALL SERVICE, MISS BUXLEY, THAT MACHINE HAS GONE HAYWIRE
MORT WALKER
4-25
© 1990 by King Features Syndicate, Inc. World rights reserved

CAN I COME IN, CHAPLAIN?
I WAS JUST LEAVING FOR LUNCH, BEETLE
I'LL WAIT
WHAT WAS IT YOU WANTED?
SANCTUARY
MORT WALKER 4-26

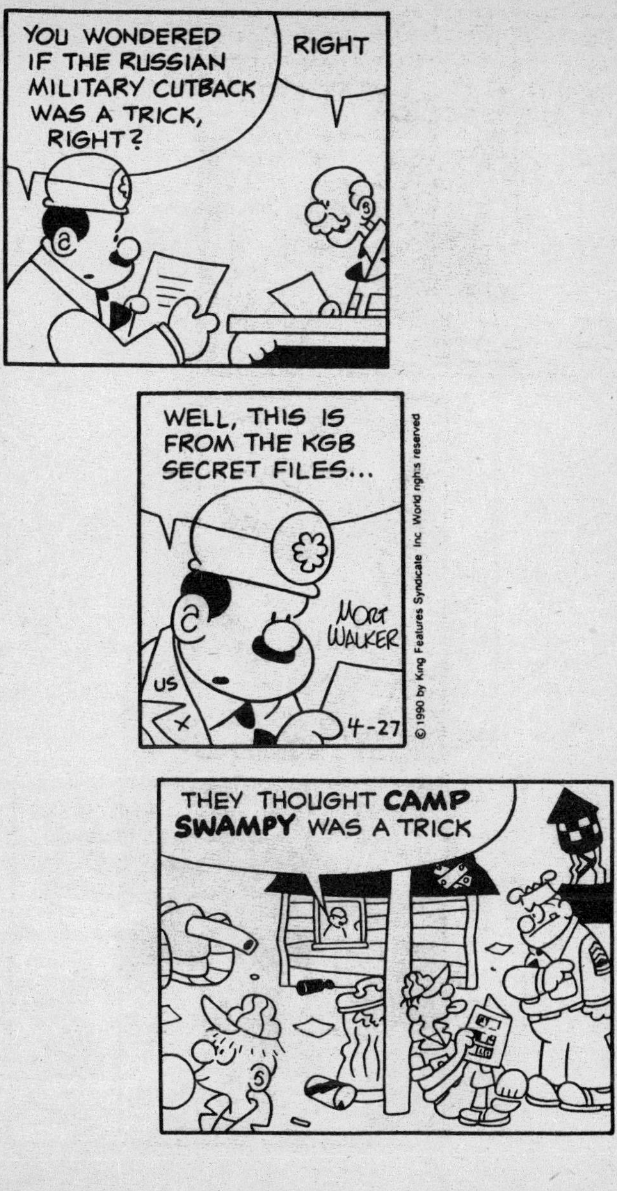
YOU WONDERED IF THE RUSSIAN MILITARY CUTBACK WAS A TRICK, RIGHT?
RIGHT
WELL, THIS IS FROM THE KGB SECRET FILES...
MORT WALKER
US
4-27
THEY THOUGHT **CAMP SWAMPY** WAS A TRICK

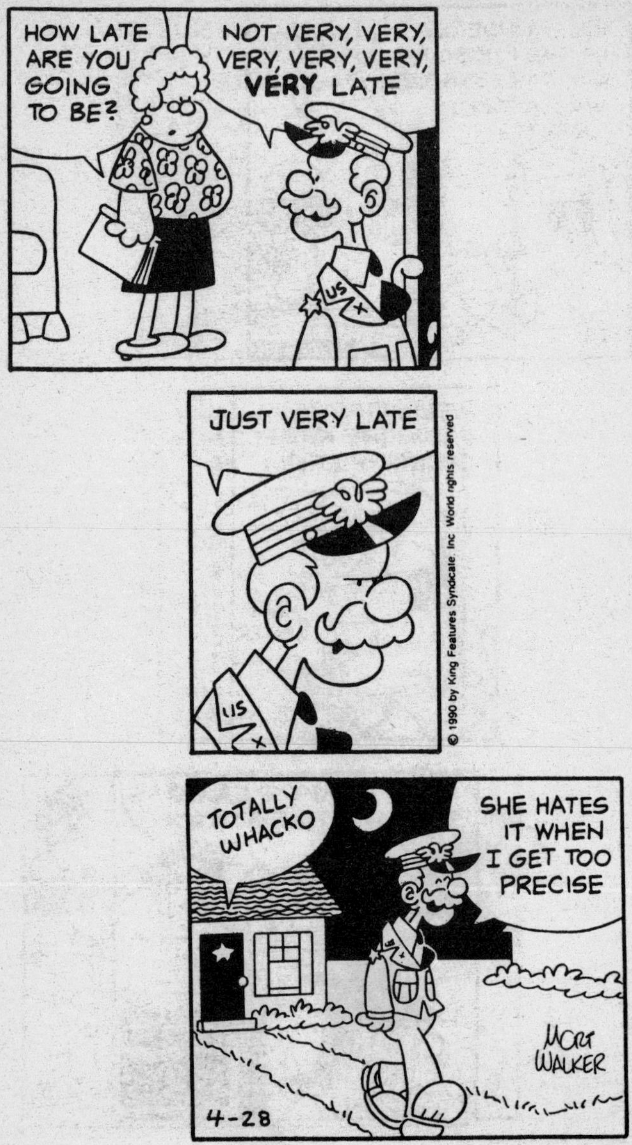
HOW LATE ARE YOU GOING TO BE?
NOT VERY, VERY, VERY, VERY, VERY, **VERY** LATE
JUST VERY LATE
TOTALLY WHACKO
SHE HATES IT WHEN I GET TOO PRECISE
MORT WALKER
4-28

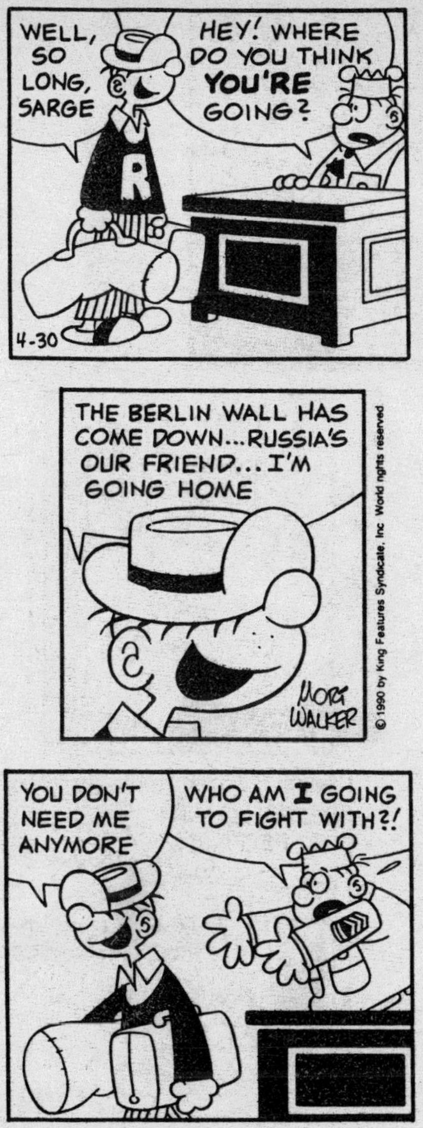
WELL, SO LONG, SARGE
HEY! WHERE DO YOU THINK YOU'RE GOING?
4-30
THE BERLIN WALL HAS COME DOWN...RUSSIA'S OUR FRIEND... I'M GOING HOME
MORT WALKER
© 1990 by King Features Syndicate, Inc. World rights reserved
YOU DON'T NEED ME ANYMORE
WHO AM I GOING TO FIGHT WITH?!

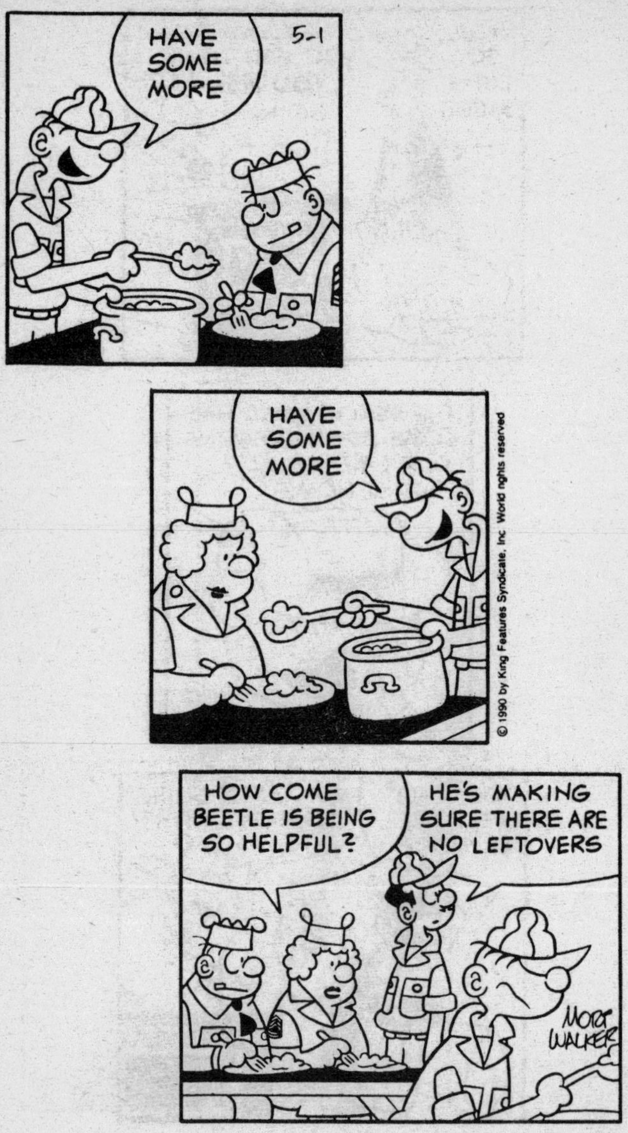
5-1
HAVE SOME MORE
HAVE SOME MORE
HOW COME BEETLE IS BEING SO HELPFUL?
HE'S MAKING SURE THERE ARE NO LEFTOVERS
MORT WALKER

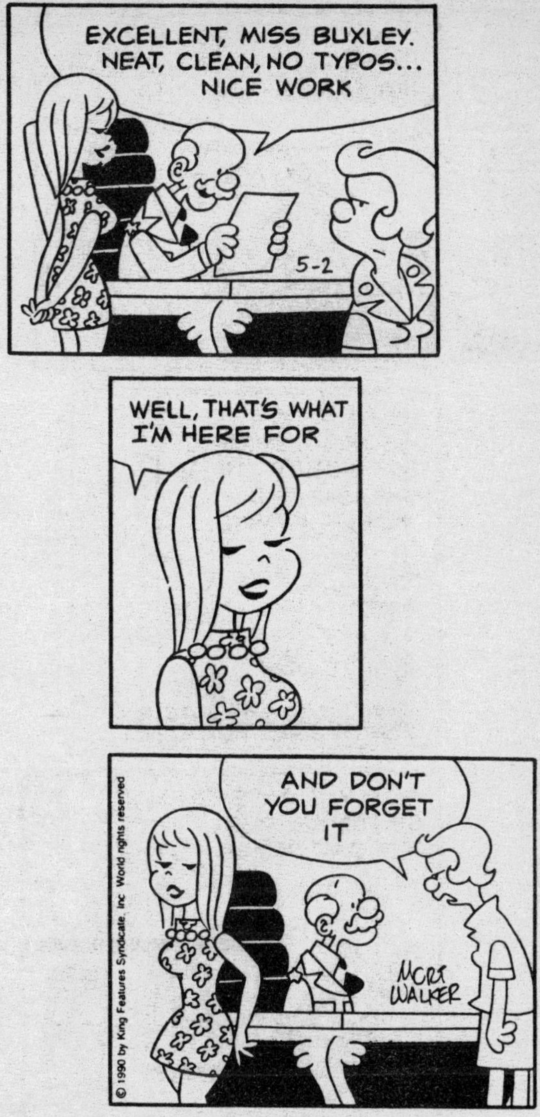
EXCELLENT, MISS BUXLEY. NEAT, CLEAN, NO TYPOS... NICE WORK
5-2
WELL, THAT'S WHAT I'M HERE FOR
AND DON'T YOU FORGET IT
© 1990 by King Features Syndicate, Inc. World rights reserved
MORT WALKER

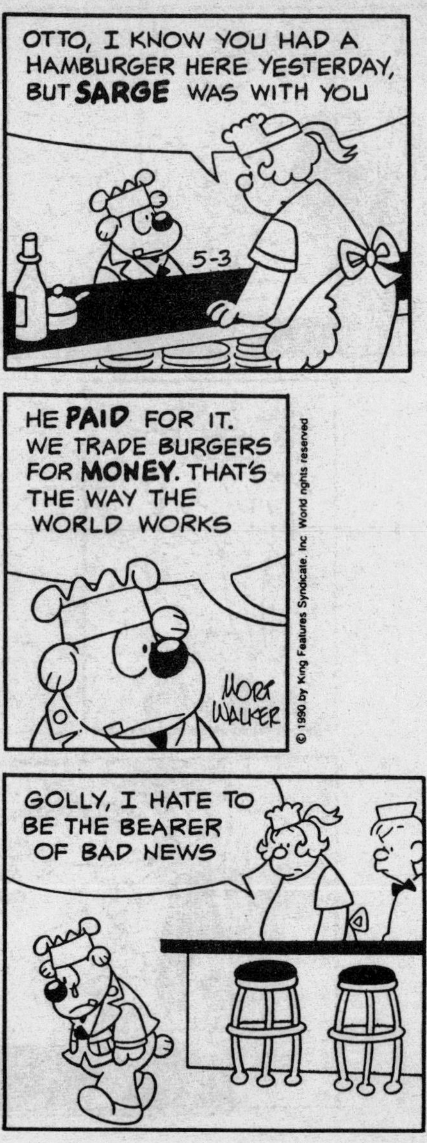
OTTO, I KNOW YOU HAD A HAMBURGER HERE YESTERDAY, BUT SARGE WAS WITH YOU
5-3
HE PAID FOR IT. WE TRADE BURGERS FOR MONEY. THAT'S THE WAY THE WORLD WORKS
MORT WALKER
GOLLY, I HATE TO BE THE BEARER OF BAD NEWS

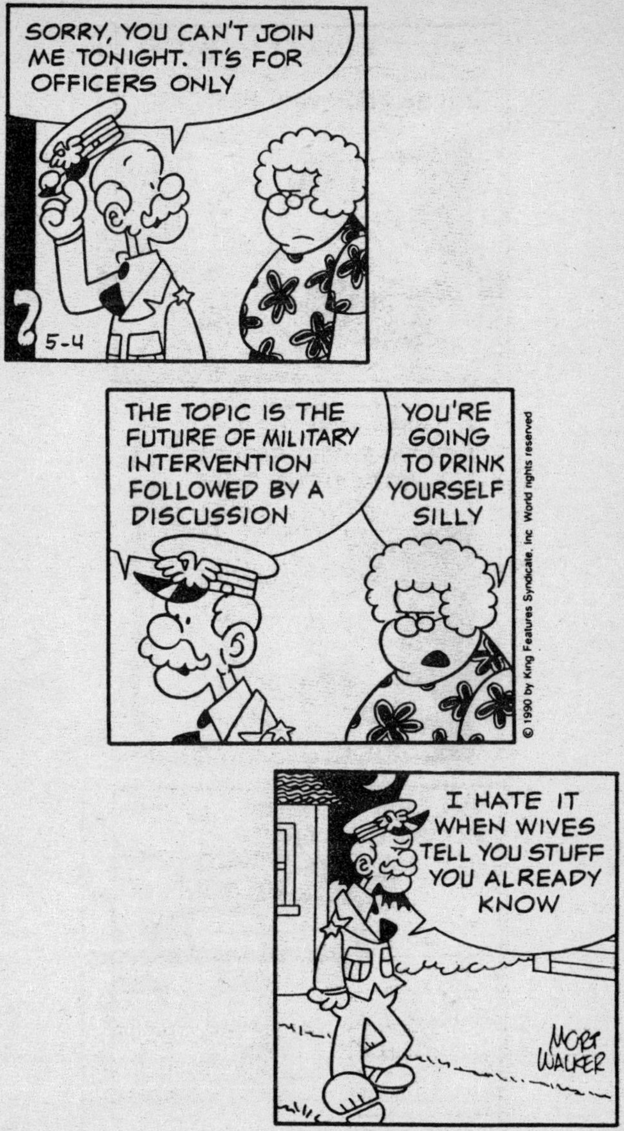
SORRY, YOU CAN'T JOIN ME TONIGHT. IT'S FOR OFFICERS ONLY
5-4
THE TOPIC IS THE FUTURE OF MILITARY INTERVENTION FOLLOWED BY A DISCUSSION
YOU'RE GOING TO DRINK YOURSELF SILLY
I HATE IT WHEN WIVES TELL YOU STUFF YOU ALREADY KNOW
MORT WALKER

I WISH WE HADN'T ACCEPTED THE INVITATION TO VISIT LOUISE LUGG AND HER CAT
5-5
I WISH I WERE SMART ENOUGH TO FIGURE A WAY OUT OF THIS
WELL, LET'S GO, OTTO
OTTO?
MORT WALKER

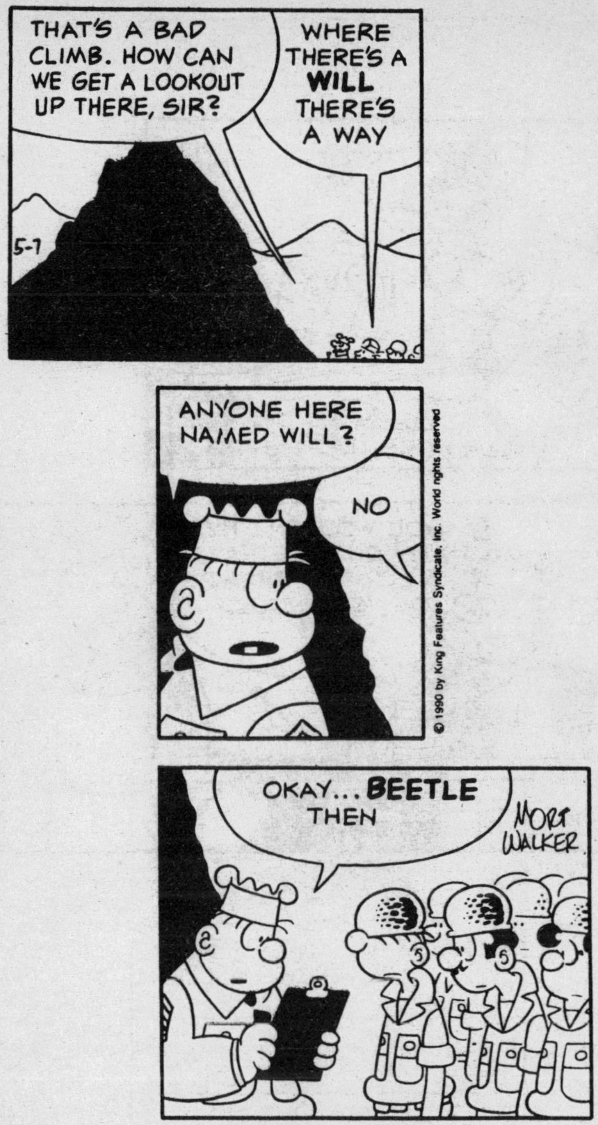
THAT'S A BAD CLIMB. HOW CAN WE GET A LOOKOUT UP THERE, SIR?
WHERE THERE'S A **WILL** THERE'S A WAY
5-7
ANYONE HERE NAMED WILL?
NO
OKAY... **BEETLE** THEN
MORT WALKER

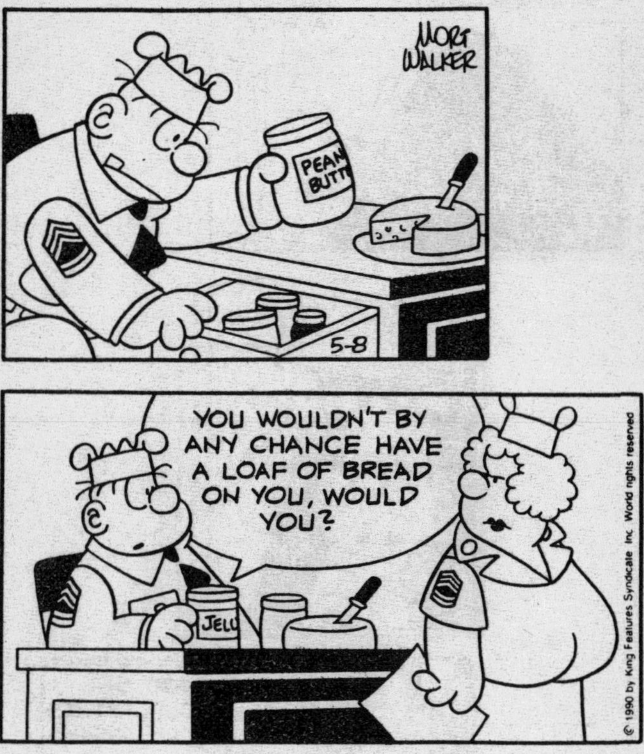
MORT WALKER
PEAN BUTT
5-8
YOU WOULDN'T BY ANY CHANCE HAVE A LOAF OF BREAD ON YOU, WOULD YOU?
JELL
© 1990 by King Features Syndicate, Inc. World rights reserved

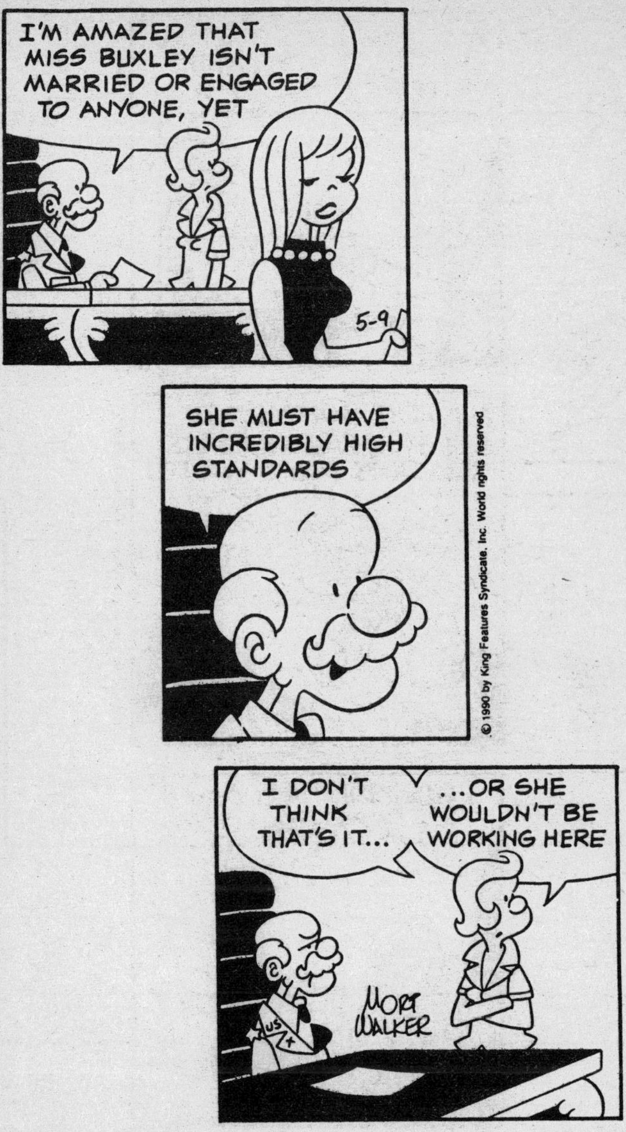
I'M AMAZED THAT MISS BUXLEY ISN'T MARRIED OR ENGAGED TO ANYONE, YET
5-9
SHE MUST HAVE INCREDIBLY HIGH STANDARDS
I DON'T THINK THAT'S IT...
...OR SHE WOULDN'T BE WORKING HERE
MORT WALKER

POST THIS ON THE BULLETIN BOARD
YOU DIDN'T SAY "PLEASE"
5-10
BLAST IT, WOMAN! I'M THE GENERAL AND I'LL TALK ANY WAY I WANT!! NOW POST IT!!
MORT WALKER
PLEASE
YOU DON'T LOOK SORRY

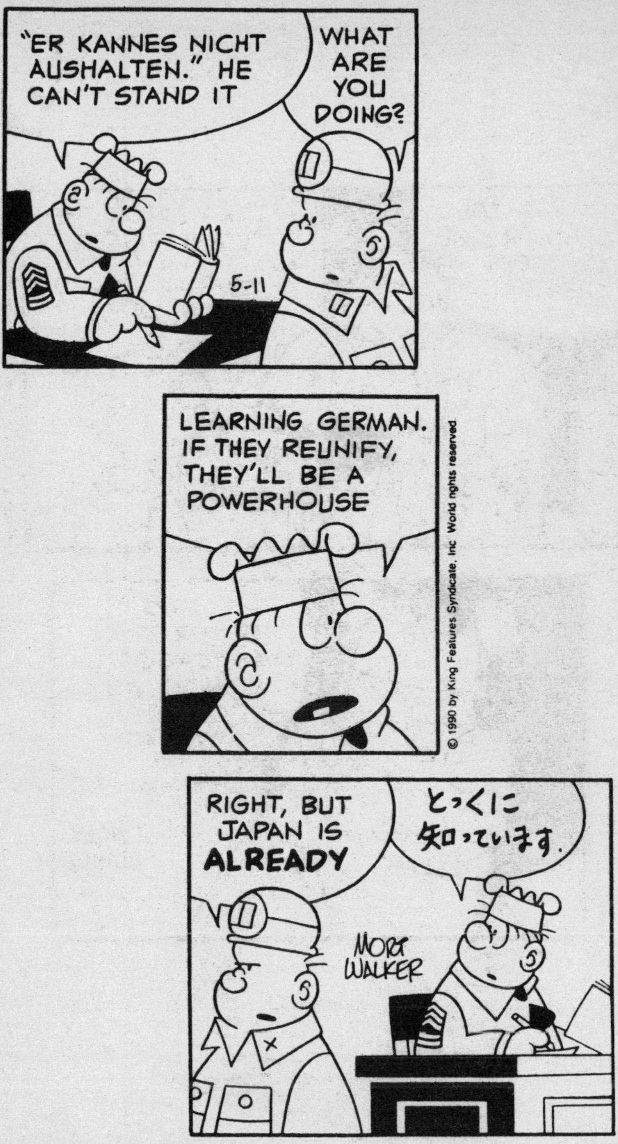
"ER KANNES NICHT AUSHALTEN." HE CAN'T STAND IT
WHAT ARE YOU DOING?
5-11
LEARNING GERMAN. IF THEY REUNIFY, THEY'LL BE A POWERHOUSE
RIGHT, BUT JAPAN IS **ALREADY**
とっくに 知っています.
MORT WALKER

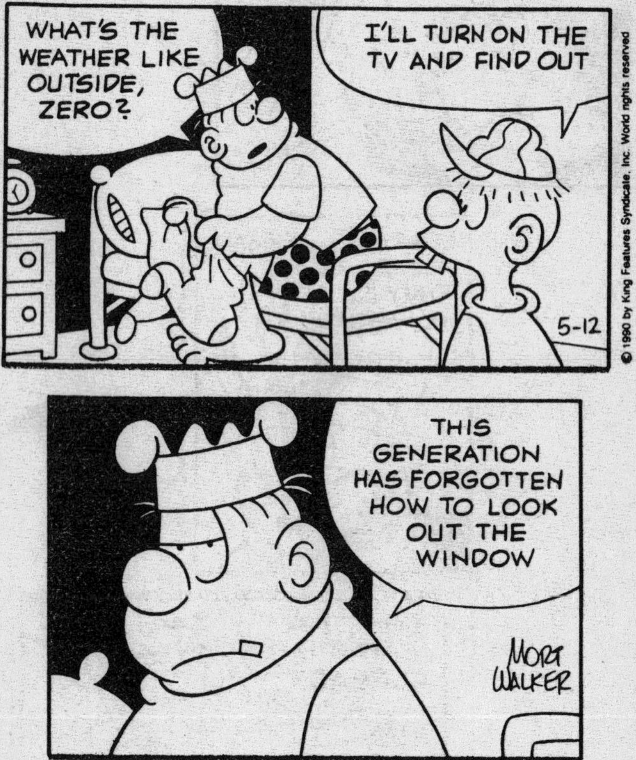
WHAT'S THE WEATHER LIKE OUTSIDE, ZERO?
I'LL TURN ON THE TV AND FIND OUT
5-12
© 1990 by King Features Syndicate, Inc. World rights reserved
THIS GENERATION HAS FORGOTTEN HOW TO LOOK OUT THE WINDOW
MORT WALKER

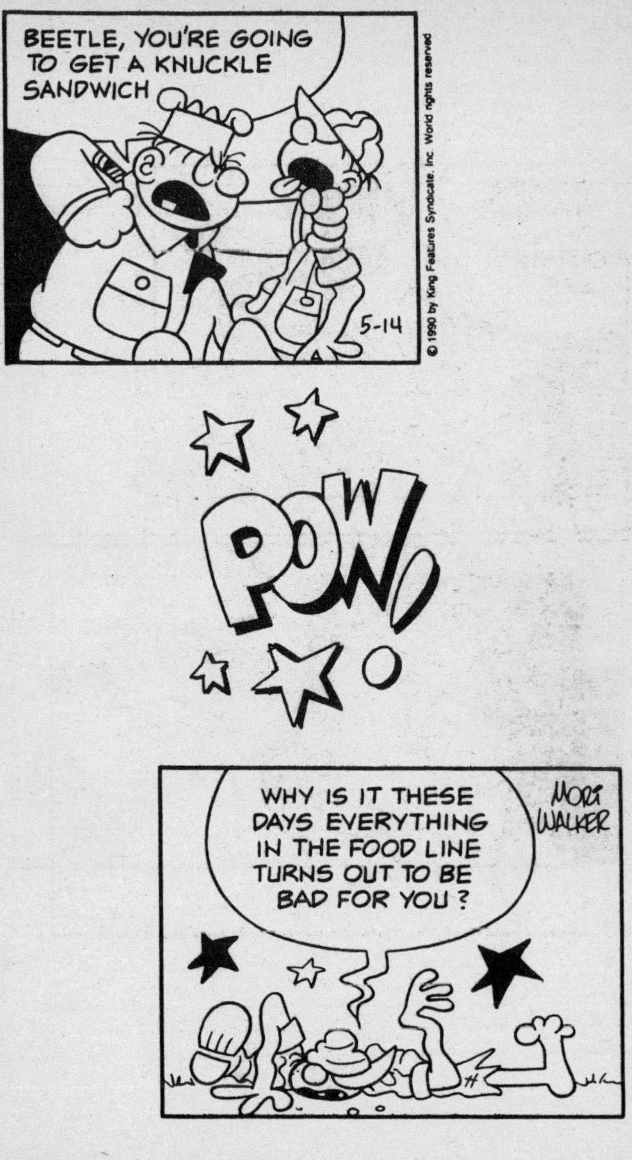
BEETLE, YOU'RE GOING TO GET A KNUCKLE SANDWICH
5-14
POW!
WHY IS IT THESE DAYS EVERYTHING IN THE FOOD LINE TURNS OUT TO BE BAD FOR YOU ?
MORT WALKER

WHERE'S THE SOAP?
I GAVE IT TO ZERO
5-15
© 1990 by King Features Syndicate, Inc. World rights reserved.
COULD I HAVE A WHACK AT THE SOAP BEFORE IT'S GONE, ZERO?
MORT WALKER

THESE DAYS, EVERYWHERE YOU LOOK, YOU SEE JOGGERS
5-16
PLUS AN OCCASIONAL DOG-TROTTER
MORT WALKER

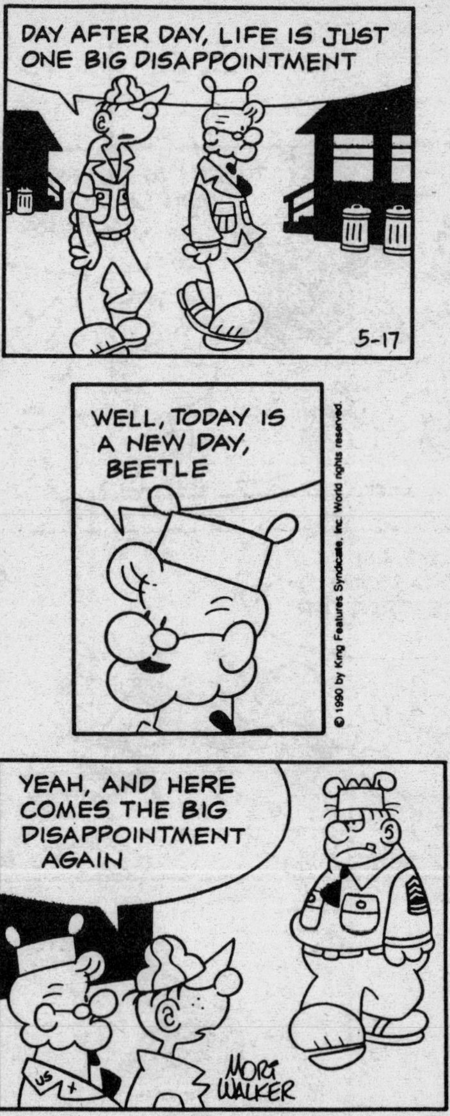
DAY AFTER DAY, LIFE IS JUST ONE BIG DISAPPOINTMENT
5-17
WELL, TODAY IS A NEW DAY, BEETLE
YEAH, AND HERE COMES THE BIG DISAPPOINTMENT AGAIN
MORT WALKER

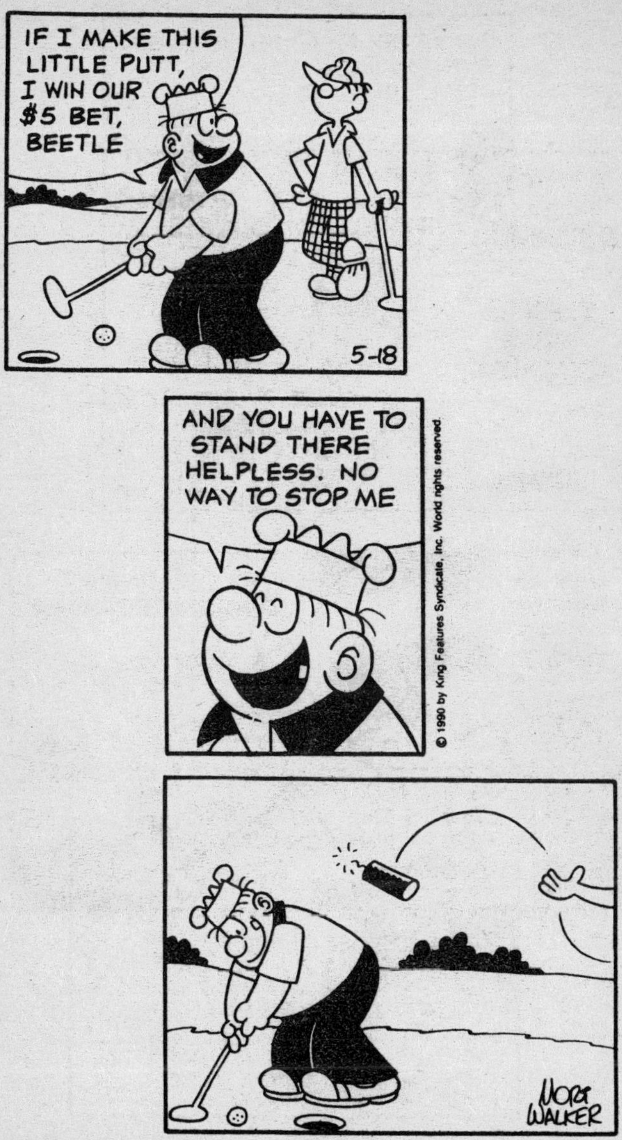
IF I MAKE THIS LITTLE PUTT, I WIN OUR $5 BET, BEETLE
5-18
AND YOU HAVE TO STAND THERE HELPLESS. NO WAY TO STOP ME
MORT WALKER

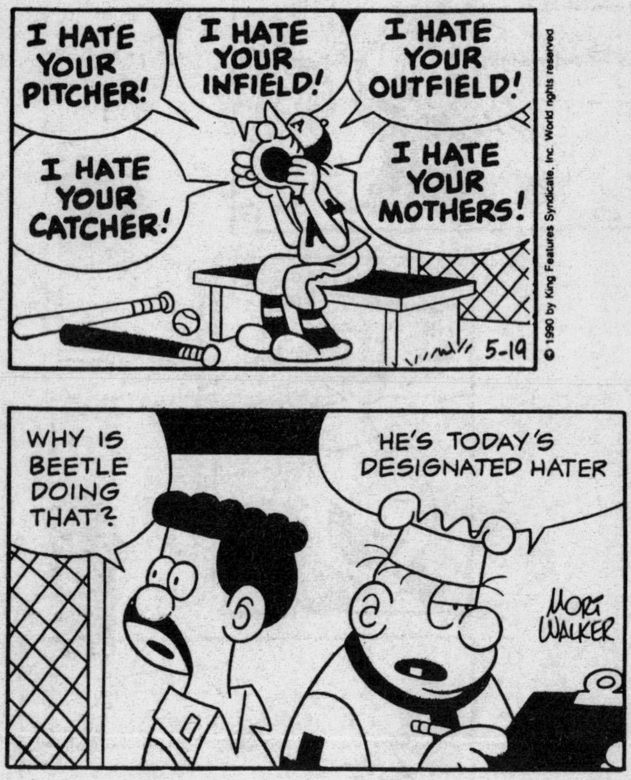
I HATE YOUR PITCHER!
I HATE YOUR INFIELD!
I HATE YOUR OUTFIELD!
I HATE YOUR CATCHER!
I HATE YOUR MOTHERS!
5-19
© 1990 by King Features Syndicate, Inc. World rights reserved
WHY IS BEETLE DOING THAT?
HE'S TODAY'S DESIGNATED HATER
MORT WALKER

WANT TO JOIN THE PHOTO CLUB, BEETLE?
NO, THANKS, SIR. I'VE JOINED TOO MANY THINGS ALREADY
5-21
LIKE WHAT?
THE ARMY
MORT WALKER

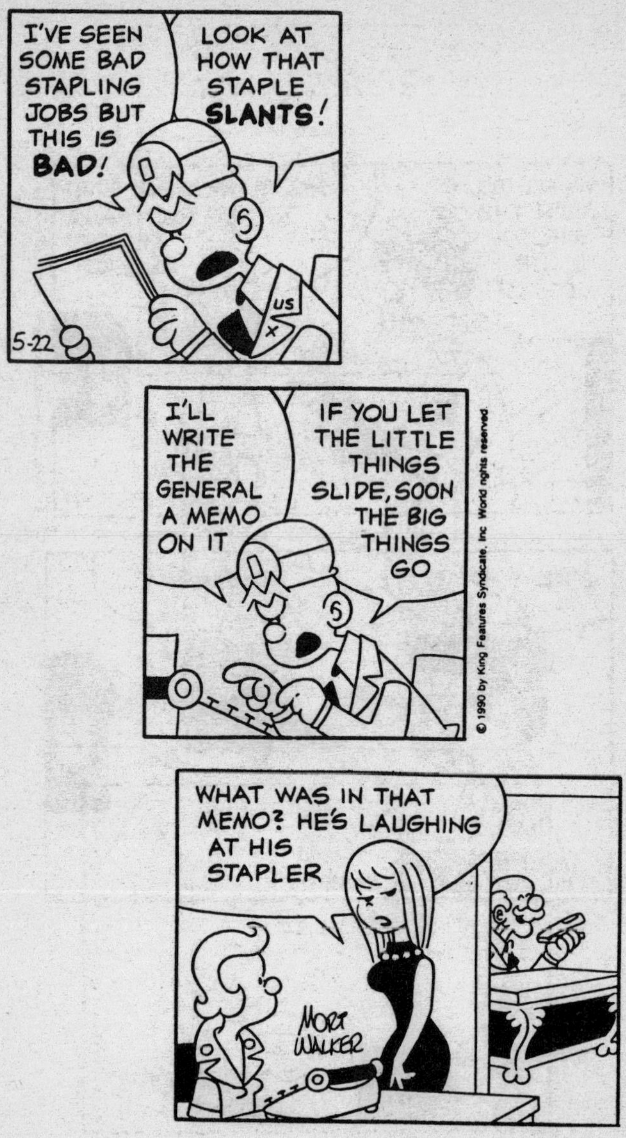
I'VE SEEN SOME BAD STAPLING JOBS BUT THIS IS **BAD**!
LOOK AT HOW THAT STAPLE **SLANTS**!
5-22
I'LL WRITE THE GENERAL A MEMO ON IT
IF YOU LET THE LITTLE THINGS SLIDE, SOON THE BIG THINGS GO
WHAT WAS IN THAT MEMO? HE'S LAUGHING AT HIS STAPLER
MORT WALKER

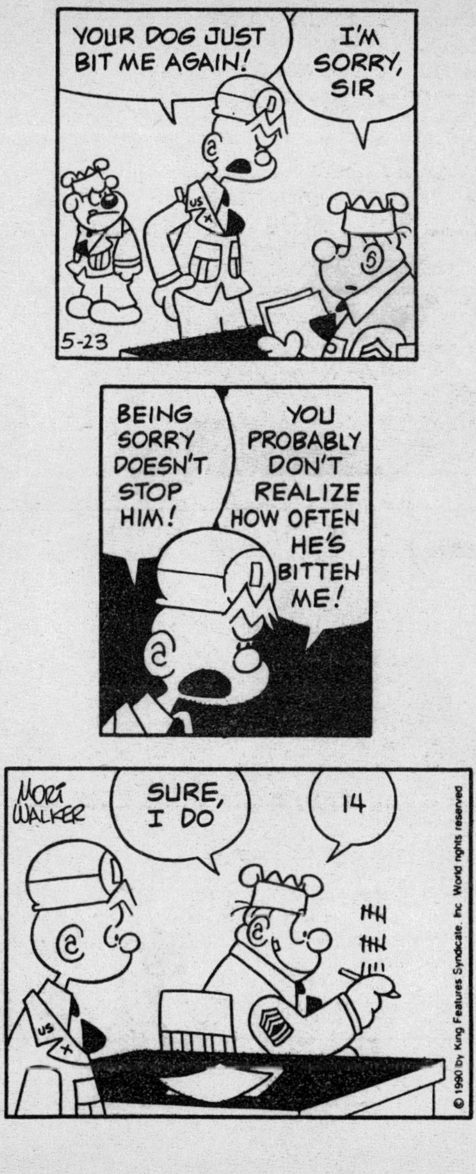
YOUR DOG JUST BIT ME AGAIN!
I'M SORRY, SIR
5-23
BEING SORRY DOESN'T STOP HIM!
YOU PROBABLY DON'T REALIZE HOW OFTEN HE'S BITTEN ME!
MORT WALKER
SURE, I DO
14
© 1990 by King Features Syndicate, Inc. World rights reserved

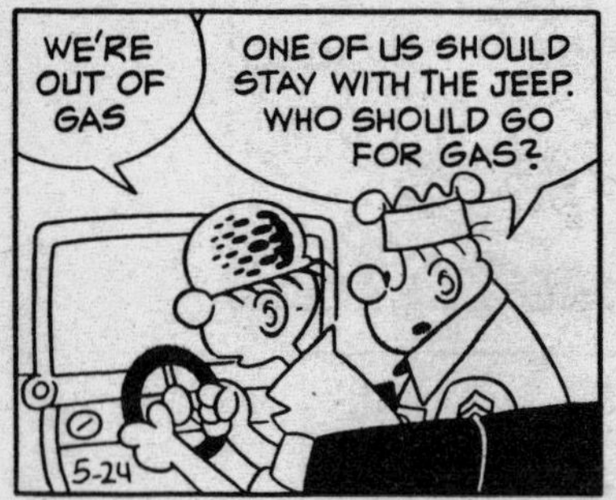
WE'RE OUT OF GAS
ONE OF US SHOULD STAY WITH THE JEEP. WHO SHOULD GO FOR GAS?
5-24

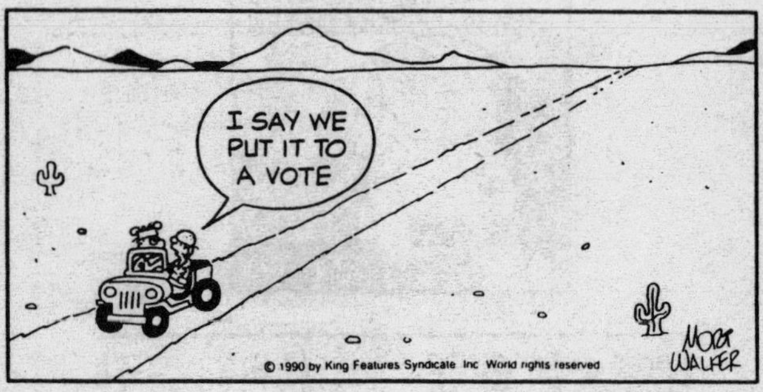
I SAY WE PUT IT TO A VOTE
© 1990 by King Features Syndicate Inc World rights reserved
MORT WALKER

"TO STOP SWAYING WHEN YOU SWING, VISUALIZE YOURSELF STANDING IN A BARREL"
5-25
GOLF TIPS
US
WHAT ARE YOU DOING?
I HAVE TROUBLE VISUALIZING
1
MORT WALKER
© 1990 by King Features Syndicate, Inc. World rights reserved

I SEE LONDON, I SEE FRANCE, I SEE SARGE'S UNDERPANTS
5-26
THAT'S ONE THING ABOUT SGT. LUGG, SHE CALLS THEM AS SHE SEES THEM
MORT WALKER

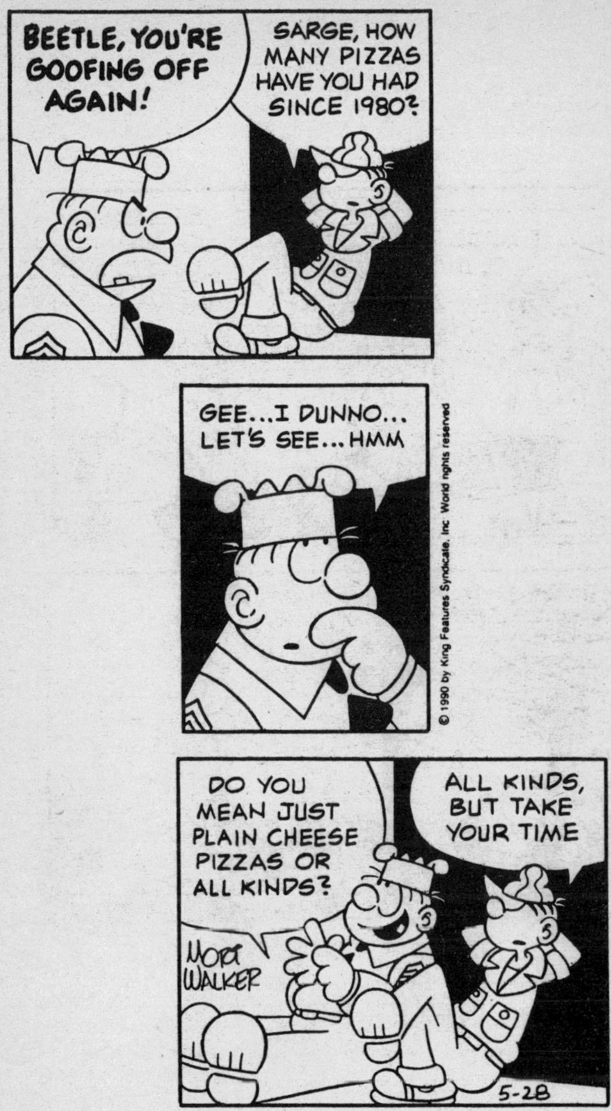
BEETLE, YOU'RE GOOFING OFF AGAIN!
SARGE, HOW MANY PIZZAS HAVE YOU HAD SINCE 1980?
GEE...I DUNNO... LET'S SEE...HMM
DO YOU MEAN JUST PLAIN CHEESE PIZZAS OR ALL KINDS?
ALL KINDS, BUT TAKE YOUR TIME
MORT WALKER
5-28

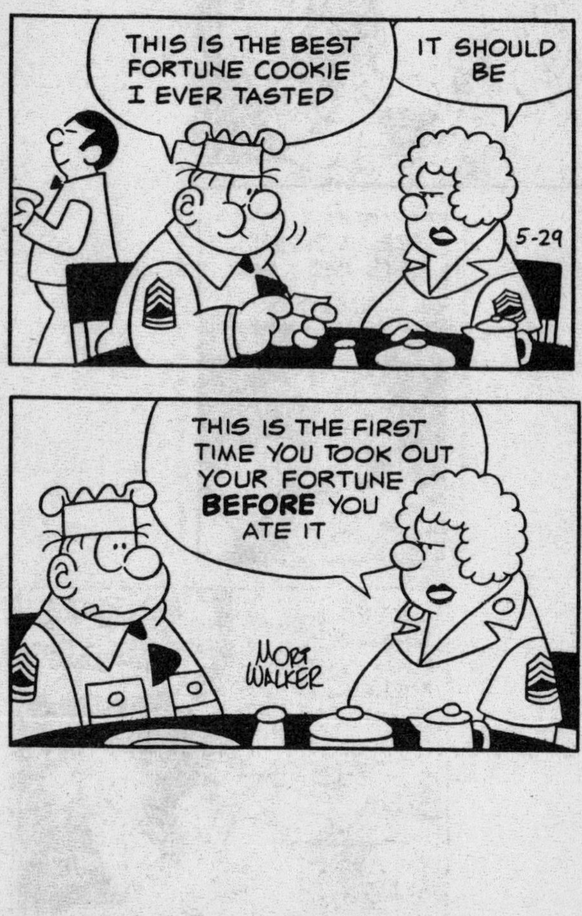
THIS IS THE BEST FORTUNE COOKIE I EVER TASTED
IT SHOULD BE
5-29
THIS IS THE FIRST TIME YOU TOOK OUT YOUR FORTUNE **BEFORE** YOU ATE IT
MORT WALKER

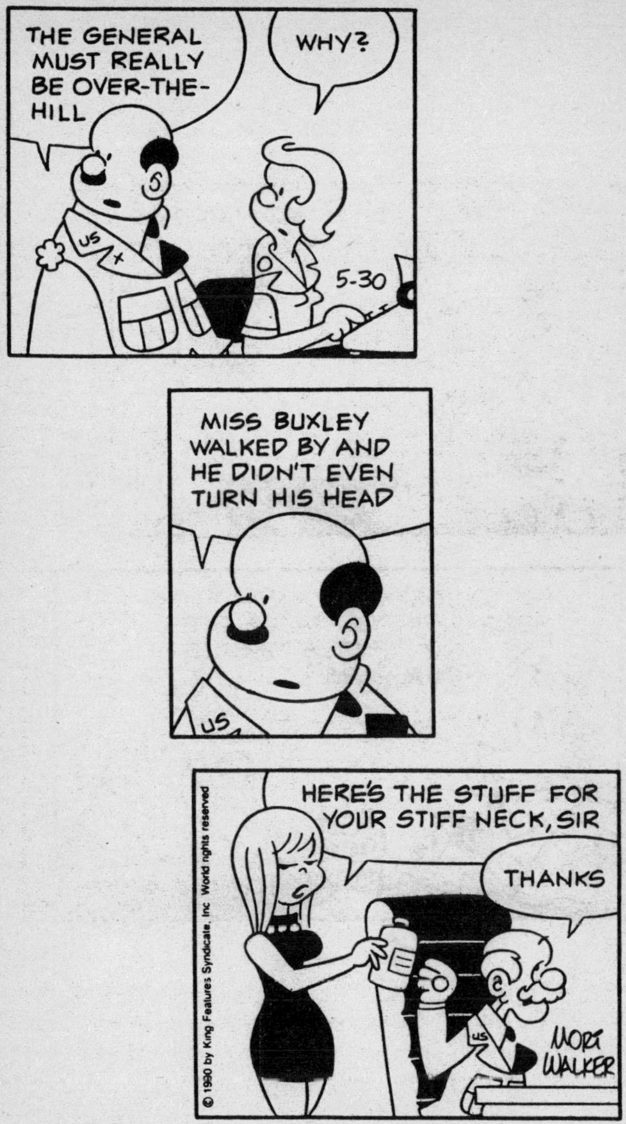
THE GENERAL MUST REALLY BE OVER-THE-HILL
WHY?
5-30
MISS BUXLEY WALKED BY AND HE DIDN'T EVEN TURN HIS HEAD
HERE'S THE STUFF FOR YOUR STIFF NECK, SIR
THANKS
© 1990 by King Features Syndicate, Inc. World rights reserved
MORT WALKER

ZERO, YOUR STUPIDITY HAS REALLY GOTTEN TO ME
NO KIDDING?
5-31
DO YOU GET AN ECHO IN YOUR HEAD WHEN YOU TALK? DOES THE WIND WHISTLE THROUGH YOUR EARS?...
MORT WALKER

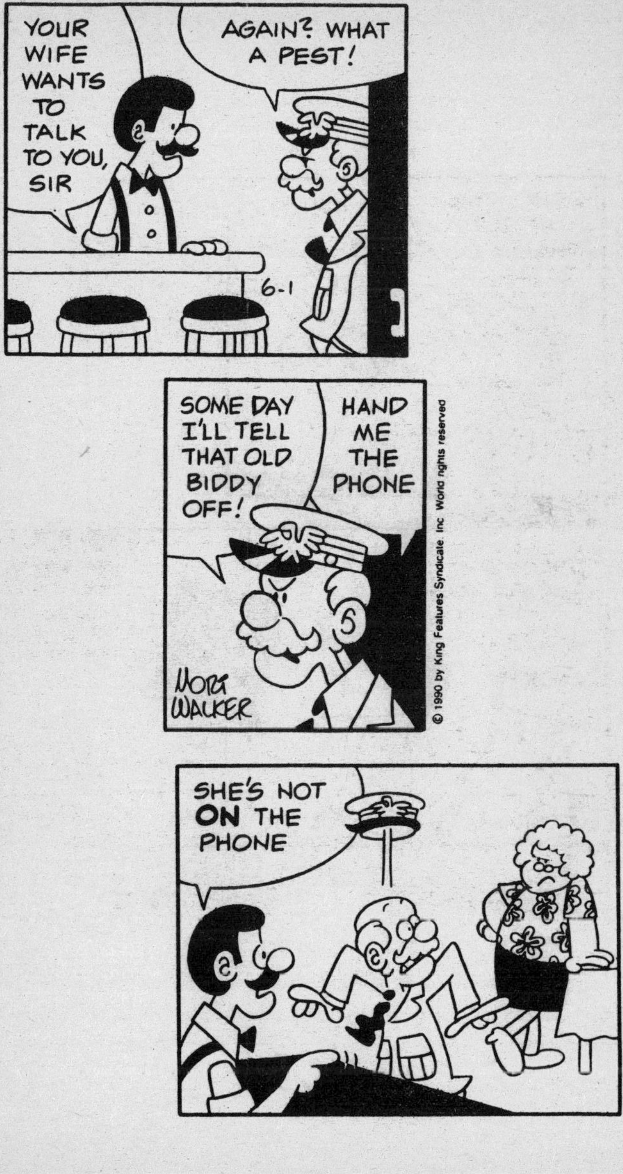
YOUR WIFE WANTS TO TALK TO YOU, SIR
AGAIN? WHAT A PEST!
6-1
SOME DAY I'LL TELL THAT OLD BIDDY OFF!
HAND ME THE PHONE
MORT WALKER
SHE'S NOT **ON** THE PHONE

OH-OH! LET'S EAT AT THE PX TONIGHT!
RIGHT!
6-2
I'M GLAD WE SET UP THIS EARLY-WARNING SYSTEM
MORT WALKER
© 1990 by King Features Syndicate, Inc. World rights reserved

LOAFING AGAIN, BEETLE! NOW YOU'RE GOING TO GET IT!
THAT'S IT, YOU BIG BULLY! GO AHEAD AND PICK ON ME!
6-4
OKAY, BUT REMEMBER, IT WAS **YOUR** IDEA
MORT WALKER

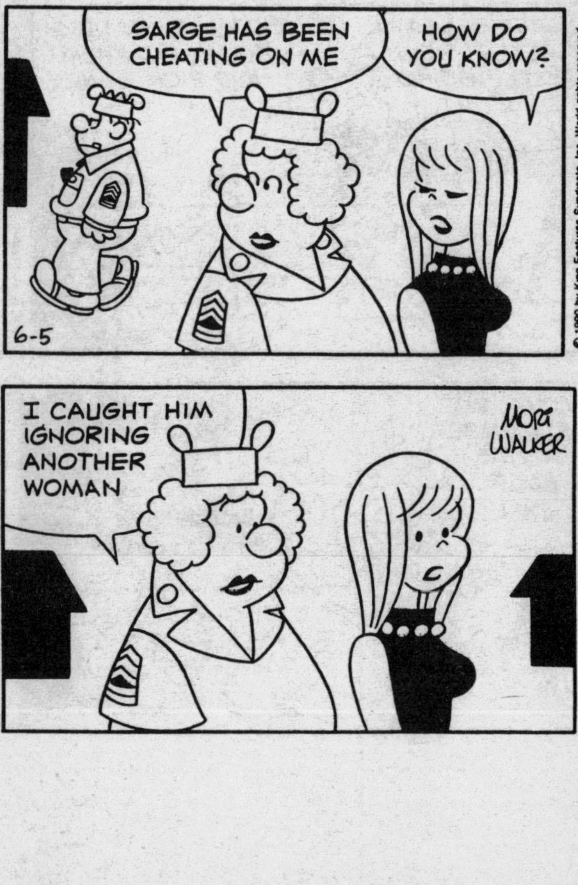
SARGE HAS BEEN CHEATING ON ME
HOW DO YOU KNOW?
6-5
I CAUGHT HIM IGNORING ANOTHER WOMAN
MORT WALKER

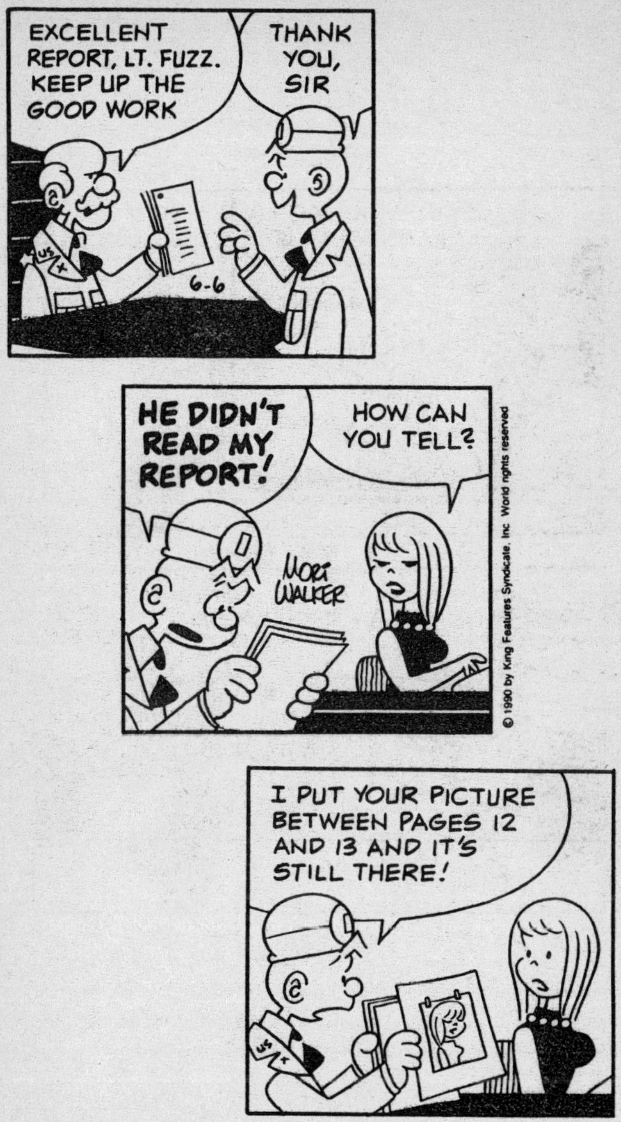

EXCELLENT REPORT, LT. FUZZ. KEEP UP THE GOOD WORK
THANK YOU, SIR
6-6
HE DIDN'T READ MY REPORT!
HOW CAN YOU TELL?
MORT WALKER
I PUT YOUR PICTURE BETWEEN PAGES 12 AND 13 AND IT'S STILL THERE!

WHY DO YOU KEEP SENDING THOSE REPORTS TO THE GENERAL?
SO WHEN A CUSHY JOB COMES UP HE'LL REMEMBER ME
© 1990 by King Features Syndicate, Inc World rights reserved
WHO WILL WE GET TO TAKE THIS MANURE SHIPMENT TO OUR DESERT BASE?
THAT PEST, LT. FUZZ
6-7
MORT WALKER

GOOD GOLLY! WHAT'S THAT?
I'M NOT SURE...
6-8
BUT OFFHAND I'D SAY IT WAS A RECONNAISSANCE BLIMP
MORT WALKER
© 1990 by King Features Syndicate Inc. World rights reserved

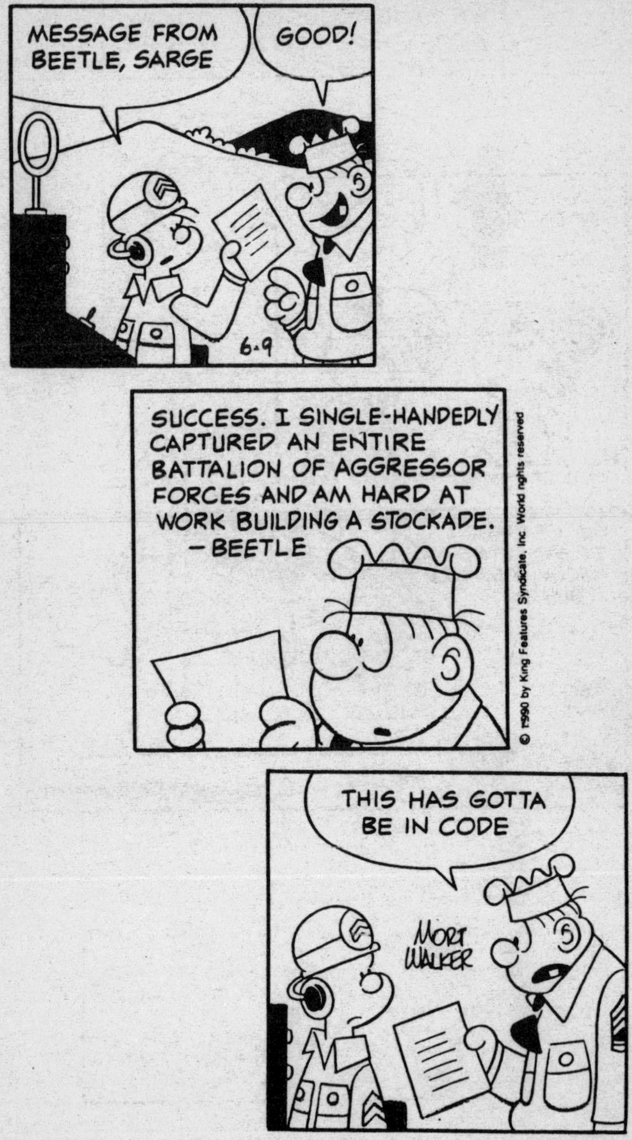
MESSAGE FROM BEETLE, SARGE
GOOD!
6-9
SUCCESS. I SINGLE-HANDEDLY CAPTURED AN ENTIRE BATTALION OF AGGRESSOR FORCES AND AM HARD AT WORK BUILDING A STOCKADE. —BEETLE
THIS HAS GOTTA BE IN CODE
MORT WALKER

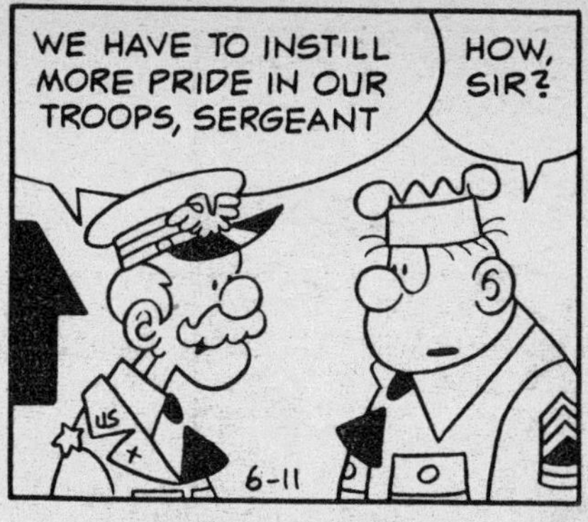
WE HAVE TO INSTILL MORE PRIDE IN OUR TROOPS, SERGEANT
HOW, SIR?
US
6-11

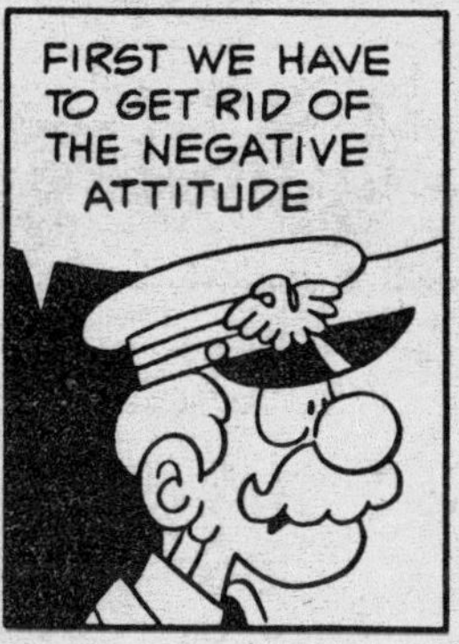
FIRST WE HAVE TO GET RID OF THE NEGATIVE ATTITUDE

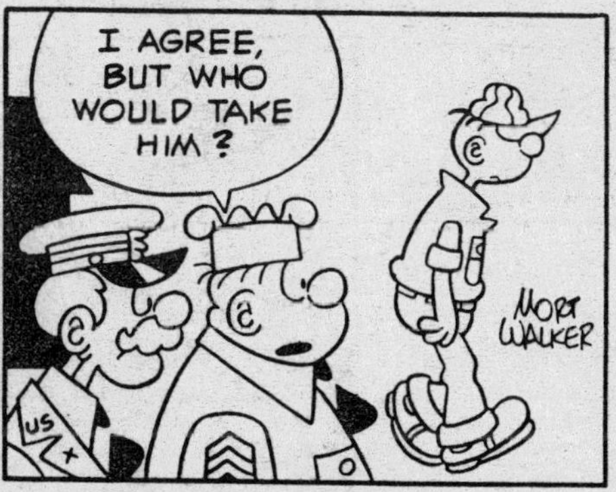
I AGREE, BUT WHO WOULD TAKE HIM?
US
MORT WALKER

BRING ME BACK A CHEESEBURGER WHILE YOU'RE IN TOWN
IT'S TEN MILES! IT'LL BE **COLD**!
6-12
IT'LL ALSO BE **GONE**
MORT WALKER

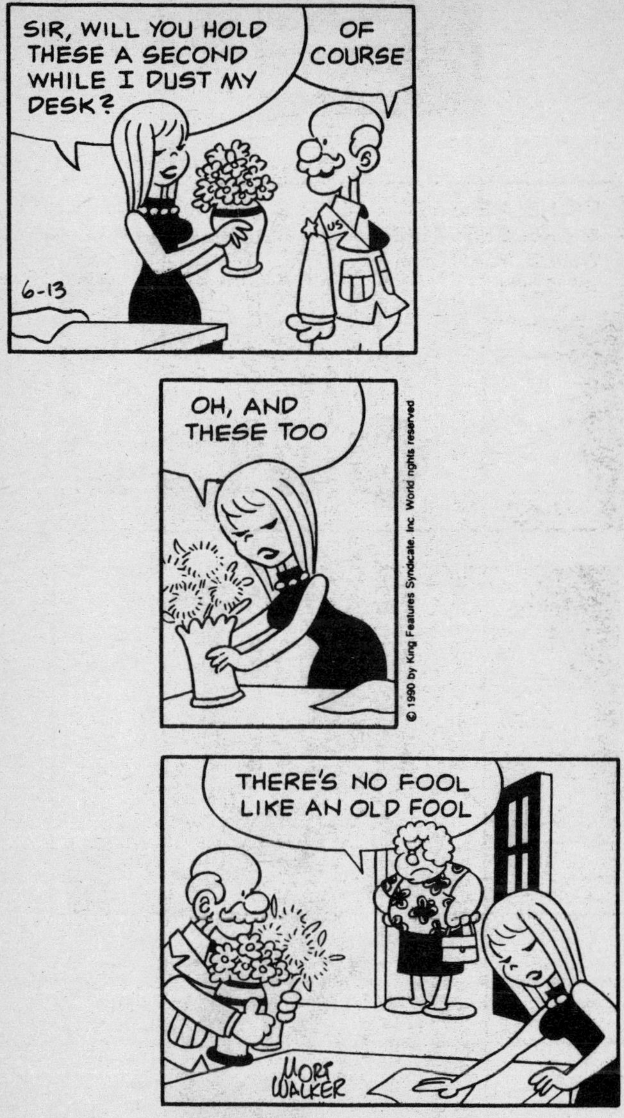
SIR, WILL YOU HOLD THESE A SECOND WHILE I DUST MY DESK?
OF COURSE
6-13
OH, AND THESE TOO
THERE'S NO FOOL LIKE AN OLD FOOL
MORT WALKER
© 1990 by King Features Syndicate, Inc. World rights reserved

I THOUGHT SARGE TOLD YOU NOT TO WRITE ON THE WALL AGAIN
EXCEPT ON FLAG DAY! HE REQUESTS IT!
THIS FLAG... THE SYMBOL OF THE HOPES OF MAN. THIS CLOTH OF DREAMS FOR FREEDOM, JUSTICE AND OPPORTUNITY. ITS STARS ARE LIKE BEACONS GUIDING US THROUGH THE SHOALS OF ADVERSITY. ITS RED STRIPES LIKE WOUNDS OF STRUGGLE. THE GOOD IN IT CANNOT BE HAD FOR NOTHING... LIKE ANY GARDEN, IT MUST BE TENDED... LIKE ANY LOVED ONE, IT MUST BE HELD. HOLD THIS FLAG HIGH AND KEEP ITS PROMISE BRIGHT, FOR IN IT LIES THE BEST HOPE FOR ALL OF US.
REPRINTED BY REQUEST
6-14
MORT WALKER

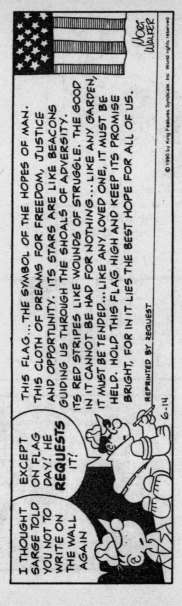

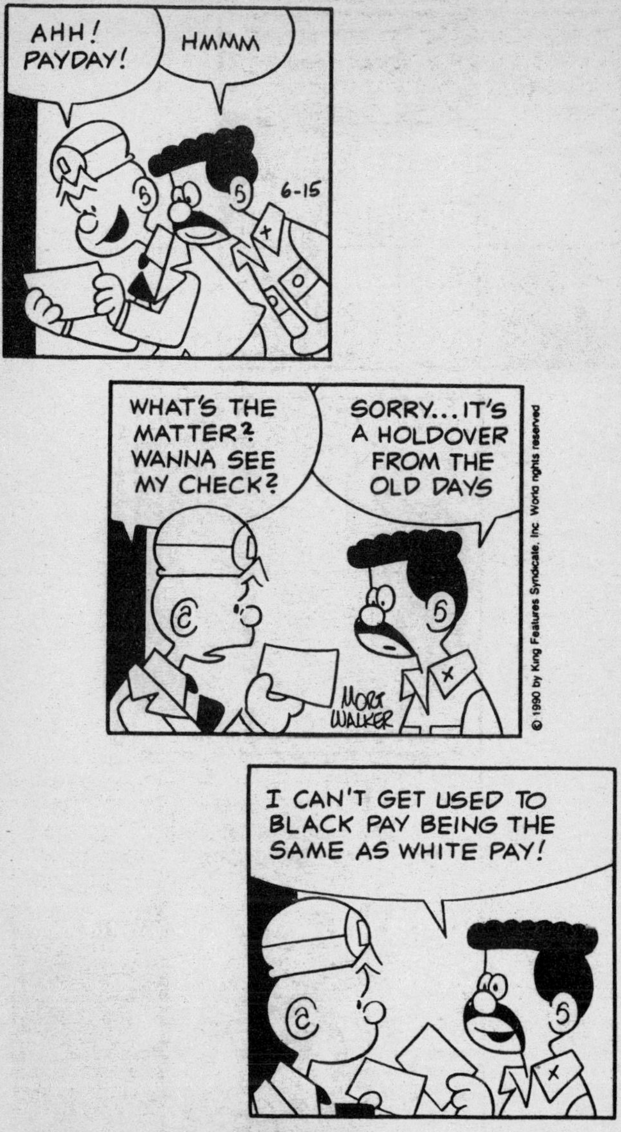
AHH! PAYDAY!
HMMM
6-15
WHAT'S THE MATTER? WANNA SEE MY CHECK?
SORRY... IT'S A HOLDOVER FROM THE OLD DAYS
MORT WALKER
© 1990 by King Features Syndicate, Inc. World rights reserved
I CAN'T GET USED TO BLACK PAY BEING THE SAME AS WHITE PAY!

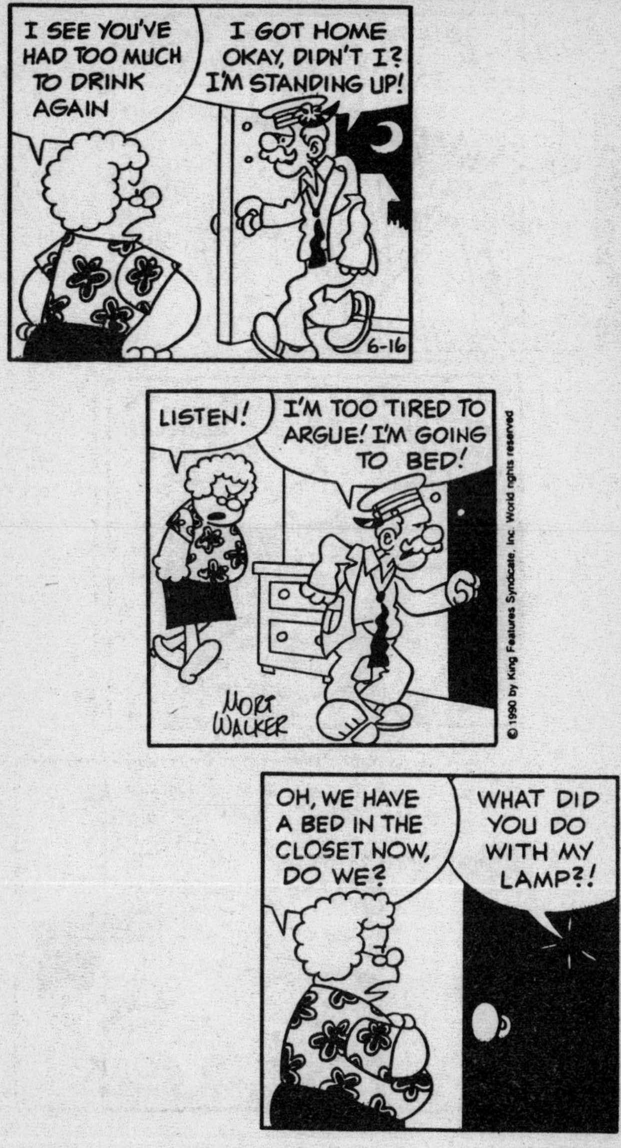
I SEE YOU'VE HAD TOO MUCH TO DRINK AGAIN
I GOT HOME OKAY, DIDN'T I? I'M STANDING UP!
6-16
LISTEN!
I'M TOO TIRED TO ARGUE! I'M GOING TO BED!
MORT WALKER
OH, WE HAVE A BED IN THE CLOSET NOW, DO WE?
WHAT DID YOU DO WITH MY LAMP?!

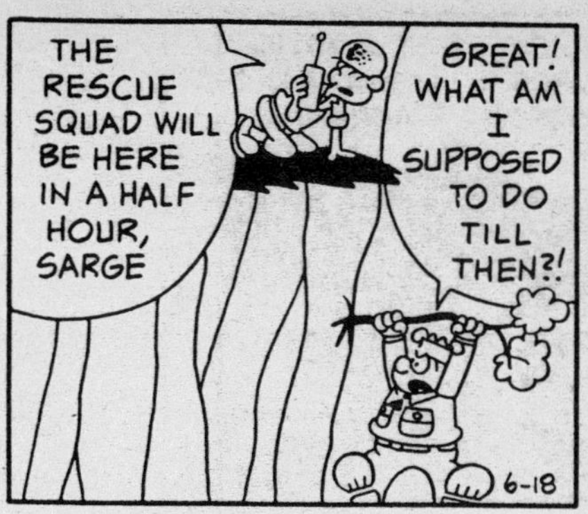
THE RESCUE SQUAD WILL BE HERE IN A HALF HOUR, SARGE
GREAT! WHAT AM I SUPPOSED TO DO TILL THEN?!
6-18

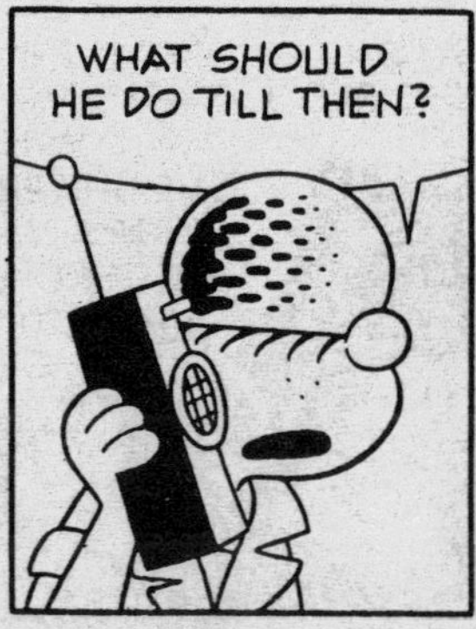
WHAT SHOULD HE DO TILL THEN?

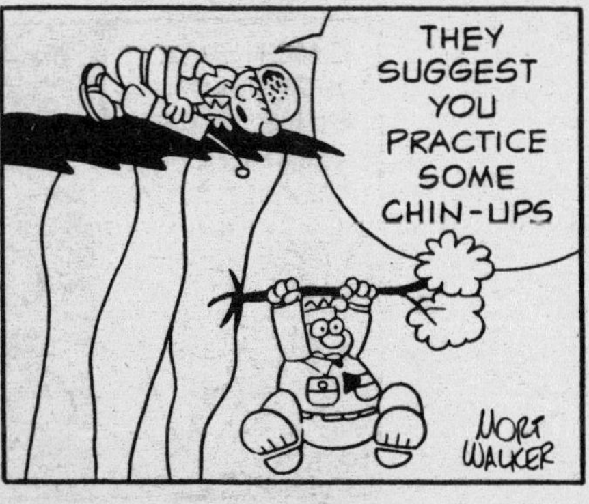
THEY SUGGEST YOU PRACTICE SOME CHIN-UPS
MORT WALKER

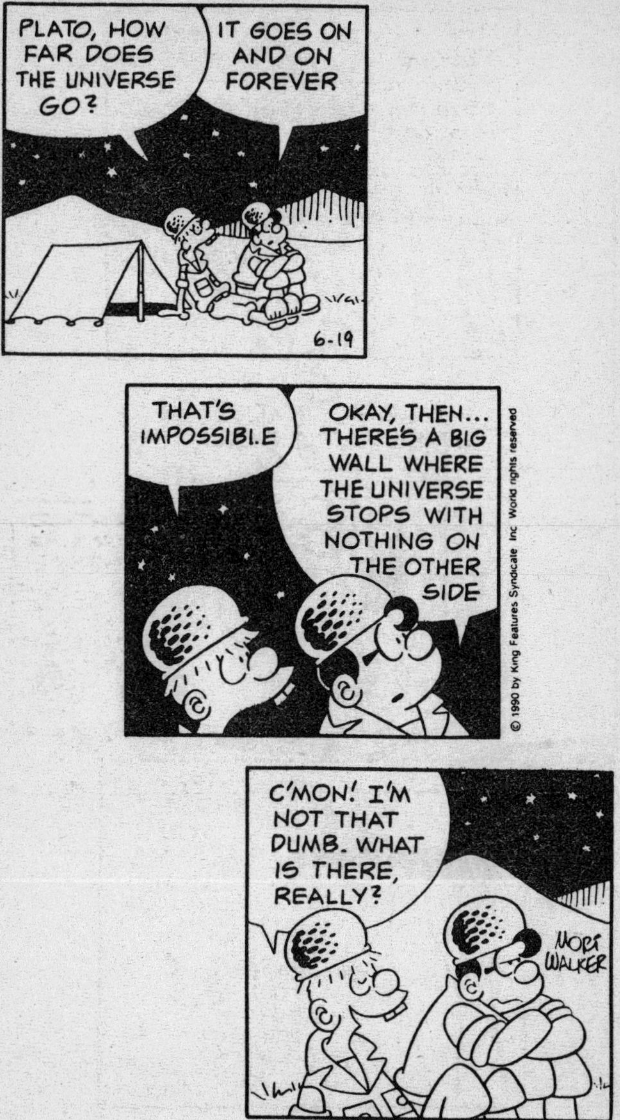
PLATO, HOW FAR DOES THE UNIVERSE GO?
IT GOES ON AND ON FOREVER
6-19
THAT'S IMPOSSIBLE
OKAY, THEN... THERE'S A BIG WALL WHERE THE UNIVERSE STOPS WITH NOTHING ON THE OTHER SIDE
C'MON! I'M NOT THAT DUMB. WHAT IS THERE, REALLY?
MORT WALKER

WHY IS THE GENERAL DOING THIS?
SOME UFO'S WERE SIGHTED IN THE AREA
6-20
WELCOME ALIENS
HE WANTS TO GET ON THEIR GOOD SIDE
NORT WALKER
© 1990 by King Features Syndicate Inc. World rights reserved

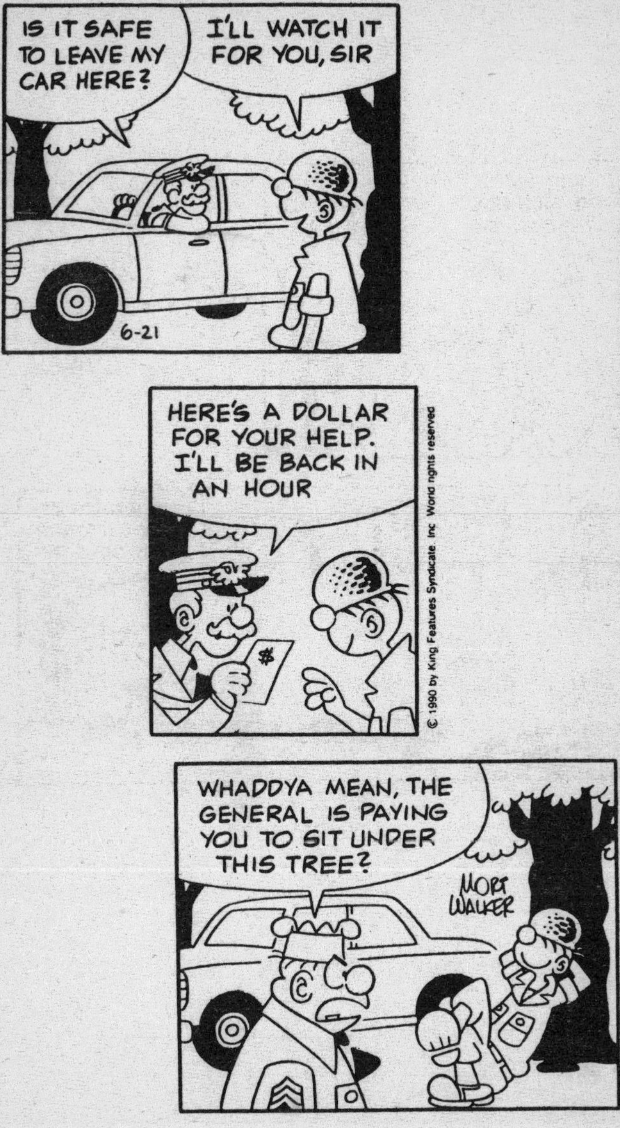
IS IT SAFE TO LEAVE MY CAR HERE?
I'LL WATCH IT FOR YOU, SIR
6-21
HERE'S A DOLLAR FOR YOUR HELP. I'LL BE BACK IN AN HOUR
$
WHADDYA MEAN, THE GENERAL IS PAYING YOU TO SIT UNDER THIS TREE?
MORT WALKER